Mastering Wall Street

David Clark,
Founder, and CEO of
Capital Strength Investments, LLC

Table of Contents

Chapter 1: Knowledge is Power 1

Chapter 2: Finding Order in Market Chaos: An Introduction to Dow Theory 19

Chapter 3: A True Understanding of Trends 45

Chapter 4: The Merits and Hazards of Technical Analysis 55

Chapter 5: What the Analysts Don't Know Can Kill You 69

Chapter 6: The Science of Madness 93

Chapter 7: Managing Money by Measuring Risk 195

Trading Rules and the Reasons Behind Them 219

Chapter 1
Knowledge is Power

People call me a trader, yet here I am writing a book primarily for investors-an apparent contradiction to those of you familiar with the distinction. So let me begin by doing what politicians never do: defining my terms. Three price trends are simultaneously active in any market: the short-term trend, which lasts from days to weeks; the intermediate-term trend, which lasts from weeks to months; and the long-term trend, which lasts from months to years. Within each market, there are three basic types of participant: traders, swing traders, and long term investors.

Traders focus their activity on the intraday and short-term trend. They buy and sell stocks, bonds, commodities, or whatever within a time frame varying from minutes to weeks. Swing traders focus on the intermediate trend, taking market positions and holding them for a period lasting from weeks to months. Investors, dealing mainly with the long term trend, hold their positions from months to years.

For most of my career, I have primarily been a swing trader. Primarily, but not solely; I play all three trends, and every transaction I make involves knowledge of each of them, so I guess that makes me a swing trader who also invests long term. For lack of a better term. I'll take the title "trader."

In my approach to the financial markets, there is an overlap of knowledge that spreads both ways from the middle; that is, the principles of swing trading apply, with some refinements, to trading and investment as well. If you understand swing trading, then it is relatively easy to shift to either trading or investing. Even more importantly, I firmly believe that the dramatic volatility in the markets that has developed over the last decade or so makes it foolish to buy and hold without understanding the importance of moving in and out of the markets or making portfolio adjustments with changes in the intermediate trend. That is why I decided to focus the subject matter on swing trading.

This book presents the essentials of my knowledge to date about the art of swing trading, which has many elements. I use the term art here in the general sense, not in the meaning of the fine arts. But just as each painter has a unique form of expression on canvas, each swing trader has a unique style of playing the markets. Still, every consistently successful market player must employ a similar set of tools: essential ideas and knowledge that guide decision making with unchanging validity. From my experience, including that gained by observing other swing traders, I have abstracted those insights for presentation to you.

A QUEST FOR FREEDOM

Freedom to me means a lot more than political liberty; it means the ability to make a living doing what I want to do, which requires maintaining a financial independence so secure that nothing short of my foolishness can take it away. Even as a teenager, the thought of relying on a paper route or a job as a bag boy at the corner grocery was tantamount to slavery in my mind. Too much of the control was out of my hands. Instead, I made money doing something I had a lot more control over. Trading individual stocks thru a company that allowed me to buy partial shares.

DISCOVERING THE NATURE OF TRENDS

To answer these questions, I first must define, measure, and classify all trends and corrections and identify a standard by which to define "normal." From 2000 until 2007, I spent almost every spare moment studying market history via Dow Theory, which gave the best definitions of market movements that I could find. Building on the work that Robert Rhea carried out until his death in 1939, I classified every trend within the Dow Industrial and Transportation averages from 1896 to the present (I keep the study current to this day) as short-term, intermediate-term, and long-term, logging their extent (how big) and duration (how long) in actuarial tables. Then, using statistical analysis, I reduced the data to terms that I can apply to my trading, specifically in risk assessment. I will discuss how I implement the data later in the book.

I point this out not for the sake of catharsis, but to make a critical point. As I note in the Preface, this book is about attaining and maintaining both financial and personal success. I failed to integrate both at that point in my life, and it was a mistake. I relate this story with the hope that it will help you avoid making similar mistakes. There is a balance in life, and the bottom line is not measured in the dollars you make, but rather to your overall happiness.

I don't want to give the impression that I use only one particularized method of analysis when making market calls. I always combine technical, statistical, and fundamental economic factors to assess the risk of any speculative position. Only when all three factors point in the same direction do I get involved in any significant way. Moreover, through experience, I have learned how crucial it is to be aware of existing or potential government intervention in the marketplace. In particular, it is vital to be aware of the effects of monetary and fiscal policy as established by Congress, the President, the Federal Reserve Board, foreign governments, and foreign central banks. You must not only understand the ejects of public policy, but you must also be able to anticipate it by understanding the character and intent of the men and women in crucial positions of power.

FINDING MY FREEDOM

"Rule No.1: Never lose money. Rule No.2: Never forget rule No.1."

-Warren Buffet

BEING EATEN ALIVE

THINKING IN ESSENTIALS

Let me provide a little motivation by showing what thinking in essentials can do for you. On the morning of Friday, October 13, 1989, traders awoke to a market that was ripe for correction. Before the market opened, most hedge funds began calling clients and the advice they were giving in essence, was the following:

I'm looking for the market to go down in a major secondary correction. Since March 23, the market has been in a sustained primary upswing. Only 2% of primary swings in all bull markets in history have lasted longer. Moreover, the Transports have appreciated 52%c in the same period. By comparison, in the 92-year history of the Industrials average, of 174 upward movements in both bull and bear markets, only eight have appreciated more than 52%c before failing. The junk bond market is falling apart there are no buyers. Further, the averages are down four days in a row from the new highs established in the Industrials on October 9, which was not confirmed by the Transports or by breadth-a definite bearish indication.

The continual upward movement in the averages and the general bullish atmosphere have been fueled by takeover and glamour stocks, while a large percentage of individual stocks have topped and are in an intermediate downtrend. The Japanese and Germans have raised interest rates; U.S. inflation is running at an annual rate of about 5.5%, and the Fed has reduced Free Reserves over the last two reporting periods relative to the previous years. I don't see any signs of the Fed easing in this atmosphere.

Consequently, I'm building a short position in the market by buying index puts; relatively small now, but if the market sells off on high volume (around 170 million shares), breaking the 2752 level on the Dow (the August high), then it is time to go short aggressively.

In the early afternoon, the market was on the way down, but on moderate volume. They were buying puts at a reasonable rate to build up their short position, expecting the market to continue to sell off into a correction the following week. The key was keeping a close eye on volume. The news broke that financing for the United Air had fallen through, and at about 2:45 PM., volume swelled, the S&P 500 Index futures started to plunge, and they began to buy puts as fast as they could. By a little after 3:00 P.m., No one could get any more orders executed-all hell had broken loose. The Industrials average closed down 191 points.

Monday morning traders expected the market to open down about 50 points or so, and most had prepared a list of stocks and options to go long if this occurred.

No one had any way of knowing that the market would close down 191 points (Figure 2.1)-the second largest drop in history-on Friday the Thirteenth or that the catalyst would be the collapse of financing for the takeover of United Airlines. Some were fortunate that the move was so large, but I wouldn't say that most were lucky to catch it. Every single analytical criterion that I use, including several that I haven't mentioned, pointed to being postured for a correction.

I will explain, as the book goes on, each component of making this kind of market call. But if I had to reduce all the elements of my methods to a single phrase, it would be thinking in essentials.

It's not necessarily how much you know, but the truth and quality of what you know that counts. Every week in Barron's there are dozens of pages of fine print summarizing the week's activities in stocks, bonds, commodities, options, and so forth. There is so much information that to process all of it, and make sense out of it, is a task beyond any genius's mental capacity.

One way to narrow down the data is to specialize in one or two areas. Another way is to use computers to do a lot of the sorting out for you. But no matter how you reduce the data, the key to processing information is the ability to abstract the essential information from the bounty of data produced each day.

To do this, you have to relate the information to principles-to fundamental concepts that define the nature of the financial markets. A principle is a broad generalization that describes an unlimited number of specific events and correlates vast amounts of data. It is with principles that you can take complex market data and make it relatively straightforward and manageable.

Take, for example, the simple statement "Savings is required for growth.'" Is this true? Is it a principle? On a common sense level, it seems self-evident that it is a principle. To buy a house, you need the money for the down payment; and to get the money for the down payment, you have to save for it. On the other hand, Keynesian economists have been telling us for years that we can deficit-finance ourselves into prosperity; that saving discourages growth, and spending is the key to continued prosperity. Who is right? What is the principle involved?

Assume for the moment that savings is required for growth and that this is true not just in a specific case such as buying a house, but for all individuals and groups engaged in economic activity-that it is a principle. What does this tell you regarding the markets? The answer is "Plenty!" It says, for example, that leveraged buyouts can't go on forever, especially when the stock market is at peak levels. A corporation with debt far exceeding the value of its cash reserves and liquid assets is especially jeopardized in a general economic decline (recession or depression). Such a company is dependent on future income or additional credit availability for its economic survival. In an economic downturn, a highly leveraged company would be hit with both decreased sales and increased credit costs. It's survival, its potential for future profitability, and therefore its value as a potential investment would be questionable if you consider the risk as well as the potential reward.

Similarly, the principle can be applied to evaluating the economy as a whole. If growth requires savings, then the producers of a nation must create more wealth than is aggregately consumed and invest the balance to produce goods and services in the future. When the federal government continually operates at a deficit, it is financing today's programs at the expense of tomorrow's products. Only one of two possibilities exist. Either (1) Americans will produce so much more in the future that the government will be able to confiscate a portion of what would have been their savings to pay the debt and still leave enough for investment; or there will be a decrease in growth, or rate of growth, as the government taxes or inflates away the existing wealth of producers. More importantly, if the government attempts to continue operating at a deficit, the attempt to spend what does not exist will eventually lead to financial disaster-a severe bear market.

Whether you agree at this point with the truth or falsehood of the principle in this example isn't the point. The example illustrates how one sentence, one bit of knowledge, leads to a whole chain of reasoning and conclusions. What initially seems enormously complex is made relatively straightforward by understanding the underlying principle.

In any endeavor, making good decisions requires the development of essential knowledge such that every observation can be related to the fundamental ideas governing the cause-and-effect relationships involved. In the financial markets, this means discovering the principles of price movements and price trends. It means understanding the nature of markets in general and defining the distinguishing characteristics that separate one market from the next.

To develop this knowledge requires a constant process of relating actual events to abstract ideas and vice versa, projecting the long term based on an analysis of today's events, and understanding today's events according to the same ideas applied in the context of both recent and history. I call this process thinking in principles, or thinking in essentials.

It is one thing to say that you should think about principles; it is quite another to identify those principles. In reading books and magazines about the financial world, you can find almost as many opinions as you can find "experts," and many of them will be diametrically opposite. Part of the reason for this is a problem of definitions. Consider some of the terms that we hear every day: bull market, bear market, trend, depression, recession, recovery, inflation, value, price, risk/reward, relative strength, and asset allocation, just to name a few. Most people in the financial world would recognize these teens, but few would be able to define them precisely. But defining them isn't just an abstract exercise; it is an essential step to understanding the markets and identifying the principles that govern them.

For the remainder of this book, I'm going to present the essentials necessary to understand the markets and profit from the knowledge-the principles of speculation that you'll need to be a successful market player.

A Business Philosophy for Consistent Success

If you read about many of the great traders in history, you'll find that a very large percentage of them blew out at least once, and some of them blew out two or three times in their career. Add to this the fact that only about 5% of commodity traders make money, and you have to wonder. "What's going on here."

There are many reasons why people lose money in the market, but one huge and easily avoided mistake is putting too much capital at risk in a single position betting it all. The error arises because people don't set forth a business philosophy for themselves before making a trade in the markets.

My objective as a trader has always been to obtain and maintain the freedom secured by financial independence: consequently, my goal has been to make money consistently, month in and month out, year after year. I have always approached this career as a business, and a prudent businessman wants first to cover his overhead each month and then concentrate on achieving a steady growth in earnings. Rather than striving for the big hit. I protect capital first and work for the consistent return, and take more aggressive risk with a portion of profits. The big hits still come along, but they come alone without excessive risk.

Translated into more practical terms. I base my business philosophy on three principles, listed here in order of importance: preservation of capital, consistent profitability, and the pursuit of superior returns. These principals are fundamental in the sense that they underlie and guide all of my market decisions. Each principle carries a different weight in my investment strategy, and they evolve from one to the other. That is, preservation of capital leads to consistent profits, which make the pursuit of superior returns possible.

PRESERVATION OF CAPITAL

Preservation of capital is the cornerstone of my business philosophy. This means that, in considering any potential market involvement. The risk is my prime concern. Before asking "What potential profit can I realize?" I first ask, "What potential loss can I suffer?" Regarding risk/reward, the maximum acceptable ratio is 1:3, the measurement of which I will discuss in this chapter and later chapters. When the risk/reward of remaining in any market is poor, I go into cash, regardless of the contemporary wisdom.

Consequently, I don't concern myself with "outperforming the averages." I work for absolute not relative returns.

In my terms, money isn't green; it's either black or white. Black and white have come to be associated with true or false, right or wrong, good or bad. In ethical terms, most of the society has been taught that "there are no blacks and whites-there is only gray": gray-the mixed and contradictory-the lack of absolutes. But on a ledger sheet, there is nothing but absolutes: 2 + 2 is always 4, and 2 - 6 is always -4! In a subtle way, the modern investor has been taught to accept gray by the money management community. He is encouraged to rejoice if his account goes down only 10% when the averages are down 20%-after all, he has outperformed the averages by 10%! This is B.S., plain and simple.

There is one, and only one, valid question for an investor to ask: "Have I made money?" The best insurance that the answer will always be "Yes!" is to consistently speculate or invest only when the odds are decidedly in your favor, which means keeping risk at a minimum. For example, if all your indicators lead you to conclude that the long-term trend in the stock market is approaching a top, at least for the intermediate term, then why put your portfolio at risk by being 100% invested on the long side? Why attempt to gain a few more percentage points over the T-bill yield when you risk the possibility of losing 50% or more of your portfolio value?

Referring to Figure 3.1, you can see that an investor who bought the Value Line at the lows in December 1984 and held until August

25, 1987, was up 67.9% before dividends. If the same investor held through October 5, when again there were signs of a top, then he was still up 65.9%. But if he continued to hold, then by October 19 he had lost all of his accumulated return-he was back down to a 0% return before dividends-two years and ten months' worth of profits down the tubes in just 14 days! Clearly, the risk/reward wasn't there.

Another case where I consider the risk too great to participate is to invest heavily in takeover stocks and junk bonds in the latter part of bull markets. Some people will tell you, "There is always a good deal out there, no matter what the condition of the stock market." Well, maybe so. But I have lived through and seen what bear markets are like. Stock prices drop day after day with no end in sight. Previously strong businesses are forced to liquidate assets to service their debt, and many weak and highly leveraged businesses go bankrupt. Leveraged buyouts (LBOs) are just that-leveraged-and the speculative bubble that made them popular in the eighties was bound to burst, as was indicated by the United Airlines fiasco in October 1989.

By my philosophy, the only reasonable way to be involved in an LBO near market tops is to get involved early, buy calls with a risk/reward ratio of 1:10 or better, and participate in a small way. Then before the stock price reaches the target takeover values . . . take your profit and run!

On the other hand, the ideal time to get involved in a takeover is at bear market bottoms or in the early stages of a bull market. This is where the real value is. As Robert Rhea put it, the last stage of a bear market "is caused by distress selling of sound securities, regardless of their value, by those who must find a cash market for at least a portion of their assets." The market player who avoids being invested near the top of bull markets-where he can get hurt in a panic crash-and plays the short side in bear markets can be in the position to take advantage of such distress selling. You might miss the last 10 or even 20% of the gains to be made near bull market tops (while making T-bill yields), but you'll still have your capital when the time comes to buy value with tremendous upside potential and almost no downside risk. In my view, the way to build wealth is to preserve capital, make consistent profits, and wait patiently for the right opportunity to make extraordinary gains.

CONSISTENT PROFITABILITY

Obviously, the markets aren't always at or near tops or bottoms. Generally speaking. A good speculator or investor should be able to capture between 60% and 80% of the long-term price trend (whether up or down) between bull market tops and bear market bottoms in any market. This is the period when the focus should be on making consistent profits with low risk.

Consistent profitability is a corollary of the preservation of capital. Now, what do I mean by a corollary? A corollary is an idea or a principle which is a direct consequence of another more fundamental principle. In this case, consistent profitability is a corollary of the preservation of capital because capital isn't a static quantity-it is either gained or lost. To increase wealth, you have to be consistently profitable; but to be consistently profitable, you have to preserve gains and minimize losses. Therefore, you must constantly balance the risks and rewards of each decision, scaling your risk according to accumulated profits or losses. Thereby increasing the odds of consistent success.

Suppose, for example, that you operate on a quarterly accounting basis. When entering a new quarter, any new positions should be small relative to the risk capital available because there are no profits accumulated for the period. In addition. Predefined exit points should be established at which you admit being wrong. Close out your position, and take the loss. If your first positions go against you, the size of any new position should be scaled back in proportion to your loss. That way, you never end a quarter losing all of your risk capital-you always have some left to build with. Conversely, if you make profits, you should apply a portion of the profits to your new positions while banking the balance, thus increasing your upside potential while preserving a portion of gains.

If I were a speculator with $50,000 to trade in the commodities futures markets, I would take an initial position of no more than 10% of the total-$5000 set exit points to limit potential losses to 10 to 20% of that-a $500 to $1000 loss. In other words, I would set it up so that my losses were no more than 1% to 2% of the total risk capital. Upon losing $1000 in the first trade. I would scale back my next opening position to $4000 and limit my losses to somewhere in the $400 to $800 range. And so forth.

On the upside, if I made $2000 on my first trade, I would bank $1000 and increase the opening size of my next position to

$6000, in effect reducing my initial capital at risk ($5000) by 20%, while increasing my actual risk capital by the same amount. That way, even if I lost on my next trade, I would still be up money for the period. Assuming that I was right in my market calls 50% of the time, I would make a lot of money by employing this strategy. And I would make a respectable living being right on only one out of three trades, provided I maintained a risk/reward ratio of, at most, 1:3. In other words, if you pick opportunities so that the probable reward is at least three times greater than the objectively measurable potential loss, you will make profits consistently over time.

Anyone who enters the financial markets expecting to be right on most of their trades is in for a rude awakening. If you think about it, it's a lot like hitting a baseball-the best players only get hits 30% to 40% of the time. But a good player knows that the hits usually help a lot more than the strikeouts hurt. The reward is greater than the risk.

This concept of constantly balancing risk/reward to keep the odds in your favor applies no matter what trend you are involved in. For example, when I day trade the S&P futures, the smallest movement I am interested in is one where I can select spots to limit losses to between three and five ticks (a tick is equal to $25 per contract), while the nearest resistance or support levels on the profitable side are a minimum of 15 to 20 ticks away. If I were looking for an intermediate movement, I would apply the same principles but with different dimensions, such as one to three points of risk versus three to ten or more points of profit.

PURSUIT OF SUPERIOR RETURNS

As profits accrue, I apply the same reasoning but take the process a step further to the pursuit of superior returns. If, and only if, a level of profits exists to justify the aggressive risk, then I will take on a higher risk to produce greater percentage returns on capital. This does not mean that I change my risk/reward criteria; it means that I increase the size of my positions.

CONCLUSION

Preservation of capital, consistent profitability, and the pursuit of superior returns are three simple principles that, if properly understood, will guide you toward making profits in the markets. But to put these ideas into practice, much more information is needed. The best starting point is to understand the nature of market movements. And I know of no better way to discuss these ideas than to introduce a body of knowledge that I consider indispensable if one is to truly understand market behavior: Dow Theory.

Chapter 2
Finding Order in Market Chaos: An Introduction to Dow Theory

There is a new theory in science-the theory of chaos-that postulates that certain types of natural activity are chaotic and unpredictable except regarding probabilities. For example, doctors can monitor and chart a heartbeat on highly sensitive equipment, but given certain conditions, a heart will go into random fibrillation during which the heartbeat cannot be predicted or modeled mathematically. This kind of chaos is life-threatening, but ironically, researchers have found that the brain waves of a healthy mind in a state of intense concentration are chaotic, whereas those of a person with epilepsy during a seizure or a drug addict on a "high" are regular and predictable.

Weather forecasting is another area where many scientists think that chaos theory applies. The unpredictability of weather comes from what is called sensitivity to initial conditions. Mathematical models fail in weather forecasting because the slightest divergence between simulated and actual conditions multiplies in a complex chain of cause and effect relationships, giving rise to results in the model entirely different than in nature. The best, chaos theory says that meteorologists can ever do is forecast the weather within the limits of probability.

If this seems like a hopeless and futile method, it is only because I don't do it justice. By studying what gives rise to chaotic behavior, scientists believe they will find the means to prevent it in some instances and to induce it in others. The potential applications are unlimited: medical, biochemical, psychiatric, meteorological, computer, and much more. So, while admitting that certain events in nature don't follow a perfect mathematical and predictable order, chaos theory says that they can still be understood and in some cases predicted and controlled.

So it is with the financial markets. People are not machines ordered and structured by mathematics; they are beings of choice. And people are the markers.

Millions of market decisions are made each day, and the results of each one has its effect on price movements. The idea that such a complex set of components, which includes free will, can be modeled and predicted with mathematical exactness is laughable. You can never predict with absolute certainty how the collection of individuals that make up the markets will react to events nor what new conditions will arise. But there is order to the chaos, and it is the speculator's job to find it.

Market forecasting is a matter of probabilities; the risk of being wrong is always present. The best you can do is minimize risk by maximizing knowledge by understanding the original conditions that give rise to probable future events. That way, it is possible to keep the odds in your favor and to be right more often than not in making market decisions. The first step in obtaining this knowledge is to find a way to monitor the pulse of market behavior.

Dow Theory, if properly understood, is like the physician's highly sensitive heart monitor or the weather forecaster's barometer; it is

Finding Order in Market Chaos: An Introduction to Dow Theory

one tool to be used as an aid in forecasting future events within the bounds of probability. It won't tell you the causes of change, but it will indicate the symptoms that lead to change. It won't tell you exactly what is going to happen, but it will give you a general overview of what is likely to happen. As William Peter Hamilton[1] put it, "Dow theory is a commonsense method of drawing useful inferences as to future market movements from the recorded daily price fluctuations of the . . . [market] averages."

Properly considered, Dow Theory provides the essential starting point with which to analyze stock market behavior. Many of its definitions and principles apply not only to the stock market but all financial markets as well.

GOOD IDEAS OFTEN MISUNDERSTOOD

The body of ideas known as Dow Theory is a composite of the work of Charles Dow, William Peter Hamilton, and Robert Rhea. Charles Dow was the founder of Dow Jones & Company and co-founder and editor of the Wall Street Journal until his death in 1902. He originated the idea of an index of stock averages with the Dow Jones Industrial average in 1895. In 1897, he created an average index for railroad stocks on the premise that the industrial and rails indexes would be indicators for the two basic economic sectors, production, and distribution.

Dow intended the indexes to be an indicator of business activity and never himself employed them to forecast stock price movements. Although he had only five years of data to work with until his death, his observations were nevertheless remarkable in both scope and accuracy.

Dow himself never organized and formalized his ideas into a theory of economic forecasting, but a friend of his named A. J. Nelson attempted such a formalization in The ABC of Stock Speculation, published in 1902. It was Nelson who dubbed Dow's methods Dow Theory.

William Peter Hamilton, who worked under Dow, was the most articulate Dow Theory advocate of his day. After Dow's death in 1902, Hamilton continued to expound upon and refine Dow's ideas primarily through editorials in the Wall Street Journal from 1903 until his death in 1929. Also, he wrote a book called The Stock Market Barometer in 1922 in which he gave Dow Theory a somewhat more detailed and formal structure beyond the scope of what was permissible in an editorial format.

Robert Rhea, forced through injury to work from his bed from 1922 until his death in 1939, was an admirer of both Hamilton and Dow and profited handsomely by applying their principles to stock price forecasting. Through detailed study, Rhea better defined the principles and methodology of the theory and developed the first set of publicly available charts of the daily closings of the Dow Jones Industrial and Railroad averages with volume included.

Among the many contributions, Rhea made to the theory were his observations characterizing size relationships as a further indication of the future of price movements. Also, although he didn't coin the name, he discovered the concept of relative strength. His book,

Finding Order in Market Chaos: An Introduction to Dow Theory

The Dots, Theory, published by Barron's in 1932 and now out of print, synopsizes Hamilton's work and provides an excellent reference for understanding the principles of Dow Theory. In a later book, Dow Theory Applied to Business and Banking; Rhea demonstrated the consistency with which Dow Theory accurately predicted the future course of business activity.

In all his writings, Rhea emphasized that Dow Theory was designed as an aid or tool to enhance the speculator's or investor's knowledge, not as an all-encompassing, rigorous, technical theory that could be divorced from knowledge of the key market and economic conditions. Dow Theory is, by definition, a technical theory; that is, it is a method of forecasting which relies on the study of patterns of price movements to infer future price behavior. In this sense, it is the father of modern technical analysis.

After Rhea's death, Dow Theory fell into less competent hands. Men who failed to grasp the essential principles of the theory misapplied and misinterpreted it, to the point that it is now generally considered dated and of little use as a technical tool in the modern markets. This is simply not true. I performed a study applying Dow Theory's principles to the Industrial and Railroad (later Transportation) averages from 1896 to 1985 and found that Dow Theory tactics accurately captured an average of 74.5% of business expansion price movements and 62% of recession price declines from confirmation date to market peaks or bottoms, respectively.

Also, the study shows that, except for periods of World War, the stock market accurately predicted changes in the business trend with a median lead time of six months and anticipated the peaks and troughs of business cycles with a median lead time of one month. The average theoretical rate of return attained by buying and selling the Industrial and Transportation indexes according to a strict interpretation of Dow Theory from 1949 to 1985 is a 20.1 % uncompounded average annual return. To this, it should be added that Dow Theory would have had an investor short through the 1987 crash (as I was). No other forecasting method can boast such a consistent and enduring record of success. Dow Theory, therefore, warrants significant investigation by any serious speculator or investor.

THE "HYPOTHESES" OE DOW THEORY

In his book, The Dow Theory, Rhea listed what he called the "hypotheses" and "theorems" of Dow Theory. They should be termed principles and definitions because Dow Theory isn't a strict system like mathematics or the physical sciences. That aside, since so many interpretations of Dow Theory are wrong, I'm going to go right to the source. I'll present Rhea's observations in the order he gave them and in his own words.[2] For the most part, these ideas stand firm today but warrant some clarification and minor revision, which follows after each quote.

According to Rhea, Dow Theory rests on three primary hypothesis that must be accepted "without any reservation whatsoever."

Hypothesis number 1

Manipulation: Manipulation is possible in the day to day movement of the averages, and secondary reactions are subject to such an influence to a more limited degree, but the primary trend can never be manipulated.

The essence of this observation is that the stock market is too diverse and too complex for one person or group to affect prices in the market as a whole for a sustained period. It is a crucial tenet of Dow Theory because if the movement of market prices as a whole could be artfully changed according to the will of one person, looking at an average index would lose any meaning beyond deciphering what the manipulator was up to. The critical importance of Hypothesis 1 will become even more evident when we examine Hypothesis 2.

Dow, Hamilton, and Rhea all thought that the degree of manipulation in their time, both by individuals and through pools, was highly overestimated. They all thought that cries of manipulation were, predominantly, desperate attempts by people who made mistakes in speculation to explain away their errors without claiming self-responsibility.

I believe the same is true today. In the context of our modern, highly regulated markets, manipulation by individuals is practically impossible, even in the short term. Program trading, however, can be a major form of manipulation, as will be described in Chapter 6. It is still true that the primary trend cannot be manipulated in a fundamental, long-term sense, but the character of the trend can be changed, as we learned during and since the crash in October 1987. Institutional trading, because of the billions of dollars involved, can accelerate the primary trend in either direction.

Hypothesis number 2:

The Averages Discount Everything: The fluctuations of the daily closing prices of the Dow-Jones rail and industrial averages afford a composite index of all hopes, disappointments, and knowledge of everyone who knows anything about financial matters, and for that reason the effects of coming events (excluding acts of God) are always properly anticipated in their movement. The averages quickly appraise such calamities as fires and earthquakes.

In Charles Dow's terms, the same basic idea was stated as follows: The market is not like a balloon plunging hither and thither in the wind. As a whole, it represents a serious, well-considered effort on the part of far-sighted and well-informed men to adjust prices to such values as exist or which are expected to exist in the not too remote future.

The major refinement necessary to bring these observations up to date is that they apply not just to the Dow Jones Industrial and Transportation averages, but to all well-formulated market indices, including bond, currency, commodity, and options indices.

There is nothing mystical about either the discounting effect or the business forecasting value reflected in the market averages. Investors use the stock and other market exchanges to allocate their capital toward companies, commodities, or other financial instruments which they think are most likely to be profitable. They place their economic resources according to their evaluations of past performance, prospects, individual preferences, and future expectations. Ultimately, the companies and investors who best anticipate the future demand of consumers (consumers in the broadest sense, including those in the capital, wholesale, and retail markets) survive and are the most profitable. Correct investments are rewarded with profits, and incorrect investments suffer losses.

The result of the actions of speculators and investors through the financial markets is a tendency to expand profitable ventures and restrict the unprofitable. Their actions can do nothing about the past and cannot solve the problem of the limited convertibility of capital goods already in existence, but they do stop good money from being thrown after bad. The movement of the market averages is simply a manifestation of this process.

If on average, market participants failed to anticipate future business activity correctly, we would experience a continuing decline in wealth, and there would be no such thing as a sustained bull market. The fact that, on average, stock traders do adequately predict the future of business activity causes the cycle of stock price movements to lead changes in the business cycle. The time lag results from the fact that stock transactions are liquid, whereas business adjustments, because of the limited convertibility of inventories and capital goods, are not.

When Rhea stated "the effects of coming events (excluding acts of God) are always properly anticipated" (emphasis added), he meant it. But implicit in his statement is a recognition that "properly" discounting includes a divergence of opinion on the effects that present events will have on future business activity. The market averages represent optimists, pessimists, and "realists"-a full spectrum of individuals and institutions with specialized knowledge that no one person can duplicate. Rhea didn't intend to imply that market participants are always predominantly right in their interpretation of coming events, but he did mean to imply that the averages always reflect the predominance of opinion. To the practiced observer, the averages will indicate the direction and strength of the long-term trend. They will show when the markets are overbought or oversold; they will tell when the tide of opinion is changing and when the risk of involvement in the markets too big to participate in any significant way.

I added the note "excluding acts of government" to Rhea's hypothesis because government legislation, monetary and fiscal policy, and trade policy, like natural disasters, can have an immediate and dramatic impact on market price movements because they have an enormous long-term economic impact. And because government policy makers are human beings, it is impossible to always correctly anticipate what they will do. An excellent example of this occurred on July 24, 1984, when Fed Chairman Paul Volcker announced that the Fed's restrictive policy was "inappropriate." In anticipation of easier credit policies, the stock market averages made their low that day, and the new bull market began.

Hypothesis number 3:

The Theory Is Not Infallible: The Dow Theory is not a perfect system for beating the market. Its successful use as an aid in speculation requires serious study, and the summing up of evidence must be impartial. The wish must never be allowed to father the thought.

The stock market is a collection of individual human beings, and human beings are fallible. With almost every stock trade, one person is right, and another is wrong. While the averages do in fact represent the net effect, or "collective wisdom" of market participants' judgments about the future, history shows time and again that millions of people can be as wrong as one, and the stock market is no exception. The nature of the market simply allows participants to adjust and correct their errors rapidly. Any method of analysis that claims the markets are infallible is flawed at its roots.

The theory of "efficient markets" is a case in point. The main premise is that with the advent of computers, information is disseminated so fast and efficiently that it is impossible to "beat the market." This is nothing more than an extrapolation into the absurdity of Dow Theory's tenet that "the averages discount everything." It is also ridiculous. The idea that everyone receives all significant information simultaneously is absurd because everyone doesn't agree on what is "significant." Even if everyone did receive the same information simultaneously, they would respond to it according to their particular circumstances and preferences. If everyone knew the same things and responded the same way, then there would be no market! You must always remember that markets exist to facilitate exchange, and exchange is the result of differences in value preferences and differences in judgments.

The predictive value of the market indices lies in the fact that they are statistically representative of a consensus expressed with money invested in the markets. Ultimately, it is people's judgments and preferences that determine prices. If you ask floor traders what is behind a price rise in their market, many will half-jokingly respond, "More buying than selling." What that answer means is, "I don't know the reasons, but the predominance of opinion, as expressed by money changing hands on the exchange floor, is that prices are going up."

The primary task of the speculator is to identify the major active factors which drive or will change the predominant trend of market participants' opinions, and the market indices provide the best tool with which to correlate events with public opinion on financial matters. The events considered can include everything from political and economic developments to technological innovations, to fashion trends, to the earnings prospects of a particular company. Since this can only be done in the context of history, the best you can do is identify the predominant factors of the past and project them on to the future. Some factors remain constant throughout history; and in general, the fundamentals which guide opinion change slowly over time. With effort, you can abstract those fundamentals and forecast the future with a high probability of accuracy.

In Hamilton's terms, the averages are a barometer for economic forecasting. In weather forecasting, a barometer is a tool for measuring changes in atmospheric pressure. Since changing atmospheric pressure always precedes changes in weather conditions, a barometer is an invaluable tool in predicting weather changes. But the barometer in itself tells the forecaster nothing about the type or quantity of precipitation to expect, nor will it accurately correlate to exact temperature changes. Similarly, the market averages are an essential tool in economic forecasting, but a great deal of supplemental information is required to piece together the entire puzzle.

THE "THEOREMS" OF DOW THEORY

After Rhea stated the hypotheses or assumptions of Dow Theory, he went on to deduce a set of what he called "theorems" from the writings of Dow and Hamilton. Rhea published these formulations in 1932, and they are essentially accurate to this day. But they cannot be taken out of context. To better understand these formulas, I recommend obtaining a complete set of the Dow Industrial and Transport averages, including volume figures, and relating the movements of the averages to the editorials of Hamilton and Rhea, which can be found in the archives of The Wall Street Journal and Barron's. Unfortunately, there is no substitute for doing this on your own. Once you grasp the nature of Hamilton's and Rhea's thinking, you can more easily apply it to our modern context, especially if you bear in mind a few refinements which will be included in the following discussion as they apply. (Refer to Figure 4.1 throughout the discussion.)

Theorem number 1:

Dow's Three Movements: There are three movements of the averages, all of which may be in progress at the same time. The first, and most important, is the primary trend: the broad upward or downward movements known as bull or bear markets, which may be of several years duration. The second and most deceptive movement is the secondary reaction: a substantial decline in a primary bull market or a rally in a major bear market. These reactions usually last from three weeks to as many months. The third, and usually unimportant, movement is the daily fluctuation.

While accurate in Rhea's terms, Dow's three movements apply not only to the averages but any market. An easy to remember reformulation of Rhea's first theorem is:

There are three trends in the stock averages and any market: the short-term trend, lasting from days to weeks; the intermediate-term trend, lasting from weeks to months; and the long-term trend, lasting from months to years. All three trends are active all the time and may be moving in opposing directions.

The long-term trend is by far the most significant trend and the easiest to identify, classify, and understand. It is of primary concern to the investor and, to a lesser extent, the speculator. The intermediate- and short-term trends are subsidiary components of the long-term trend and can only be understood and fully taken advantage of through a recognition of their status within the long-term.

The intermediate-term trend is of secondary importance to the investor and primary importance to the speculator. It can move with the long-term trend or against it. If the intermediate-term trend significantly retraces the long-term trend, it is characterized as a secondary reaction or a correction. The characteristics of a secondary reaction must be closely evaluated to avoid confusing it with a change in the long-term trend.

The short-term trend is the least predictable and is of primary concern only to the trader. The speculator's and investor's interest in the short-term trend should consist almost solely in optimizing profits and minimizing losses by the timing of buys and sells within the short-term movement.

Classifying price changes regarding the three trends isn't just a mental exercise. The investor who is aware of the three trends focuses on the long-term trend, but depending on how hard he wants to work, he can use intermediate and short-term movements that run contrary to the primary trend to optimize profits in several ways. First, if the long-term trend is up, he may choose to benefit from a secondary reaction by selling stock short throughout the correction and then using the profits to pyramid his long position somewhere near the turning point of the correction. Second, he may do the same thing by buying puts or selling calls. Third, he may ride through the contra-move with confidence, knowing that it is an intermediate-, not a long-term, move. And finally, he may use short-term movements to time buys and sells for optimum profitability.

For the speculator, the same kind of thinking applies, except that he is not interested in holding positions through secondary reactions that move against him; his objective is to go with the intermediate-term trend in either direction. The speculator can use the short-term trend to look for signs that the intermediate-term trend is changing. The mind set is different from that of the investor, but the basic principles used to identify change are very similar.

Since the early eighties, program trading and improvements in the dissemination of information have dramatically increased the volatility of intermediate market movements. Since 1987, daily fluctuations of 50 or more points in a day have become commonplace. Because of this, I think the wisdom of the long-term "buy and hold" approach to investment is now questionable at best. To me, it seems self-evident that it is a waste to hold long positions through corrections, watching as years of gains are whittled down to almost nothing. True enough, in most cases, those gains will come back over a period of months to years. But if you focus on the intermediate-term trend, the bulk of these large losses are avoidable. I, therefore, think the primary purpose of the prudent investor should be on the intermediate-term trend.

But to accurately focus on the intermediate-term trend, you have to understand it in relation to the long-term, or primary trend.

Theorem number 2:

Primary Movements: The primary movement is the broad basic trend known as a bull or bear markets extending over periods which have varied from less than a year to several years. The correct determination of the direction of this movement is the most important factor in successful speculation. There is no known method of forecasting the extent or duration of a primary movement.

Knowing the long-term trend, or primary movement is the essential minimum requirement for successful speculation and investment. The speculator who knows and is confident of the long-term trend has enough knowledge to make a decent living, given at least minimum prudence in timing specific market selections. Although there is, in fact, no way to predict with certainty the extent or duration of a primary movement, it is possible to characterize primary movements and secondary reactions statistically using historical price movements as a database.

Rhea described all price changes in Dow history as to type, extent, and duration but had only about three decades of data to work with. Remarkably, there is little difference between the characterizations he made then, and those made now with 92 years of data. For example, the bell curve distributions of both the extents and durations of secondary reactions in both bull and bear markets, classified jointly or separately, is virtually the same now as it was when Rhea published his data in 1932; there are just more data points now.

This is remarkable because it tells us that, with all the sophistication and knowledge gained in the last half-century, it is evident that the psychology which drives market price movements is very similar over time. What this means to the professional speculator is that it is very likely that market movements will fall within a limited range of their historical extent and duration medians. If a price movement extends beyond its median levels, then the statistical risk of being involved in that trend grows each day. If carefully weighed and applied, this dimension of risk assessment can add significantly to the probability of accurately forecasting the future of price movements.'

Theorem number 3:

Primary Bear Markets: A major bear market is the long downward movement interrupted by major rallies. It is caused by various economic ills and does not terminate until stock prices have thoroughly discounted the worst that is apt to occur. There are three principal phases of a bear market: the first represents the abandonment of hopes upon which stocks were purchased at inflated prices; the second reflects selling due to decreased business and earnings, and the third is caused by distress selling of sound securities, regardless of their value, by those who must find a cash market for a least a portion of their assets.

Several aspects of this definition need to be clarified. The distinguishing characteristic of the bear market movement is that the "significant rallies," or secondary corrections, in both the Industrials and the Transports never penetrate the previous bull market top or previous intermediate highs jointly. The "economic ills" referred to are, almost without fail, the result of government action: interventionist legislation, grossly restrictive tax and trade policies, irresponsible monetary and fiscal policy, and major wars. Based on my own Dow Theory classification of the market averages from 1896 to the present, some of the key characteristics of bear markets are as follows:

1. The median extent of bear markets is a 29.4% decline from the previous bull market high, with 75% of all bear markets falling between 20.4% and 47.1%.

2. The median duration of bear markets is 1. 1 years, with 75% of all bear markets lasting between 0.8 and 2.8 years.

3. The beginnings of bear markets usually follow a "test" of the previous bull market high. On low volume followed by sharp declines in high volume. A "test" is when price levels closely approach but never reach the previous high point jointly. The low volume during this "test" is a key indication that confidence is at a low ebb and can quickly turn into an "abandonment of hopes upon which stocks were purchased at inflated prices."

4. After an extended bear swing, secondary reactions are usually marked by sudden and rapid advances followed by decreasing activity and the formation of a "line," which ultimately leads to slower declines to new lows

5. The confirmation date of a bear market is the time when prices on both the averages break below the low point of the last bull

market correction and continue to move downward. It is not atypical for one average to lag the other in time

6. Intermediate bear market rallies are usually inverted "V" patterns where the low is made on high volume, and the high is made on small volume.

Rhea made another observation about bear markets that deserves critical attention:

At the end of the bear period, the market seems to be immune to further bad news and pessimism. It also appears to have lost its ability to bounce back after severe declines and has every appearance of having reached a state of equilibrium where speculative activities are at a low ebb, where offerings do little to depress prices, but where there appears to be no demand sufficient to lift quotations. Pessimism is rampant, dividends are being passed, some prominent companies are usually in financial difficulty. Because of all these things, stocks make a "line." When this "line" is broken on the upside, the daily fluctuations of the averages show a tendency to work to a slightly higher ground on each rally, with the ensuing declines failing to pass through the last immediate low. It is then that a speculative position on the long side is indicated. This observation applies equally to the commodities markets minus, of course, the statement made about dividends.

Theorem number 4:

Primary Bull Markets: A primary bull market is a broad upward movement, interrupted by secondary reactions, and averaging longer than two years. During this time, stock prices advance because of demand created by both investment and speculative buying caused by improving business conditions and increased speculative activity. There are three phases of a bull period: the first is represented by reviving confidence in the future of business; the second is the response of stock prices to the known improvement in corporations earnings, and the third is the period when speculation is rampant and inflation apparent-a period when stocks are advanced on hopes and expectations.

This definition also needs clarification. The distinguishing characteristic of a bull market is that price movements in all major averages continue jointly to establish new high points, react in declines to low points somewhere above the lows in previous secondary reactions, and then proceed to new high points. Declines in secondary reactions do not jointly fall below the previous important market lows. Some of the major characteristics of primary bull markets are:

1. The median extent of primary bull markets is a 77.5% increase in prices from the previous bear market low point.

2. The median duration of primary bull markets is two years and four months or 2.33 years. 75% of all bull markets in history has lasted more than 657 days (1.8 years), and 67% have lasted between 1.8 and 4.1 years.

3. The beginnings of bull markets are virtually indistinguishable from the previous secondary reaction in the bear market until the passage of some time.

4. Secondary reactions in bull markets are usually marked by sharp rates of price decline relative to the preceding and ensuing price increases. Also, the beginning of the reaction is usually marked by high volume, with the lows made on low volume

5. The confirmation date of a bull market is the time when prices in both the averages break above the high point of the last bear market correction and continue to move upward.

Theorem number 5:

Secondary Reactions: for this discussion, a secondary reaction is considered to be a substantial decline in a bull market or advance in a bear market, usually lasting from three weeks to as many months, during which intervals the price movement generally retraces from 33% to 66% of the primary price change since the termination of the last preceding secondary reaction [emphasis added]. These responses are frequently erroneously assumed to represent a change of primary trend, because apparently, the first stage of a bull market must always coincide with a movement which might have proved to have been merely a secondary reaction in a bear market, the contra being real after the peak has been attained in a bull market.

A secondary reaction, or a correction, is a significant intermediate-term price movement that significantly retraces the movement of the primary trend. Determining when an intermediate movement that opposes the primary trend is "important" is the most subtle and challenging aspect of Dow Theory, and misreading such a move can be very damaging financially to the highly leveraged speculator.

Judging when an intermediate move is a correction requires looking at volume relationships, statistical data on the historical probabilities of it being a correction, the general attitude of market participants, the financial conditions of different companies, the state of the economy, the policies of the Federal Reserve Board, and many other factors. The classification is somewhat subjective, but it is critical to be accurate. Quite often, it's hard or impossible to tell the difference between a secondary reaction and the ending of a primary movement. There are, however, some important indications which will become apparent in this discussion and later chapters.

My research bears out Rhea's observation that most secondary corrections retrace from '/3 to % of the previous primary swing and last from three weeks to three months. Of all the corrections in history, 61% retraced between 30 and 70%. The first secondary reaction. The first primary swing illustrates what Rhea described as, "... reviving confidence in the future of business. The previous major swing, 65% last between three weeks and three months, and 98% last from two weeks to eight months. Another distinguishing characteristic is that the rate of change of price movements in secondary reactions are typically swifter and sharper than the flow of the primary trend.

Secondary reactions should not be confused with minor reactions that frequently occur within primary and secondary price movements. Minor reactions move in opposition to the intermediate trend and last less than two weeks (14 calendar days) 98.7% of the time. They have virtually no impact on the intermediate or long-term trends. Only nine movements lasting less than two weeks of the 694 intermediate movements (both up and down) in the history of the Transports and Industrial averages to date (October 1989) warrant classification as secondary corrections.

The key term in Rhea's definition of a secondary reaction is important. As a general rule, any movement retracing more than 1/3 of the previous primary swing is important if it occurs as a result of fundamental changes in the economy, not just technical factors. For example, if the Fed raised margin requirements from 50 to 70% in the stock market, there would be a substantial liquidation that had nothing to do with the health of the economy or of the companies whose stocks were affected. Such a movement would be minor. If on the other hand, half of California fell into the sea in a major earthquake and the market sold off 600 points in three days, the sell-off would be major because the earnings of companies would be affected.

Making the distinction between minor reactions and secondary corrections isn't always this clear-cut, however, and is the only somewhat subjective element of Dow Theory.

Rhea likened secondary reactions to the pressure control system on a boiler system. In a bull market, the secondary correction is the safety valve which relieves the pressure of an overbought market. In a bear market, the secondary reaction is a new fire in the furnace to build up strength that is lacking from an oversold condition.

CONCLUSION

Dow Theory alone is by no means the comprehensive way to forecast market behavior, but it is an invaluable component of knowledge that no prudent speculator should ignore. Many of the principles of Dow Theory are implicit in the language of Wall Street and the vocabulary of market participants without their even knowing it. For example, most market professionals have a general impression of what a correction is, but no one that I know of has defined a correction in the objective terms that Dow Theory does.

By reviewing the basic tenets of Dow Theory, we have learned a general method of gauging the future of market price movements by studying both current and historical price movements of the market averages. We now have a general idea of what a trend is. We know that three trends are simultaneously active in any market and the relative importance of each to the trader, speculator, and investor.

Bearing these ideas in mind, it is now time to gain a deeper understanding of price trends. After all, if you know what the trend is, and if you find out when it is most likely to change, then you have all the knowledge you need to make money in the markets.

Chapter 3
A True Understanding of Trends

UPTREND, DOWNTREND, MOVE ALL AROUND TREND

One of the most amazing things to me is how few people, even market professionals, understand what a trend is. For example, if someone threw Figure 5.1 at me and asked me what the trend was in gold, what do you think I would answer" The best answer would be, "Which trend are you talking about'?

When I look at this chart, I see three separate and distinct trends: the long-term trend, which is down; the intermediate trend, which is up; and the short-term trend (or the minor trend), which is down If you don't truly understand what a trend is, you can draw a trendline on a chart irtually any way you want to, and the conclusions you draw from looking at this so-called '*trendline" will be useless.

I'll demonstrate in detail how to correctly and consistently draw a trendline in a later chapter for now, let's gain some broader insights into what a trend is exactly, and how it changes.

LET'S REDUCE-IT TO BASICS

Probably the single most important piece of information you can get from Dole', Theory is the definition of a trend, which is implied but never clearly stated, and the distinction between the long-term, intermediate-term, and short-term trends. It is only by understanding what a trend is that you can determine when a change of trend occurs, and it is only by accurately identifying a change of trend that you can accurately time your buys and sells to maximize profits and minimize losses in any market. From Dow Theory, I have abstracted the following definitions:

The upward Trend-An upward trend is a series of successive rallies that penetrate previous high points, interrupted by sell-offs or declines which terminate above the weak points of the preceding sell-off. In other words, an uptrend is a price movement consisting of a series of higher highs and higher lows.

Downward Trend-A downward trend is a series of consecutive declines which penetrate previous weak points, interrupted by rallies or increases which terminate below the high points of the preceding rally. In other words, a downtrend is a price movement consisting of a series of lower lows and lower highs

If you learn anything from this book, learn these definitions. They are very, very simple but also of crucial importance. These definitions are completely general in that they apply to any market and to any period. I think it is simple to see from the hypothetical figures that following the trend is the way to make money in the financial markets. What is not quite clear in the definitions is how you determine where the previous high and low points are. This depends totally on whether you're focusing your trading activities in the short-term, intermediate-term, or long-term trend that is, whether you are trading, speculating, or investing.

A True Understanding of Trends

No matter what market or what period you participate in, you won't make money (except by luck) unless you know the direction of the trend and how to identify a change of trend. While Dow Theory is still fresh on your mind, some additional observations from it can be instrumental. A few of these observations apply only to the equities markets, but most of them apply to any market. Understanding them is of tremendous help in identifying when a change of trend is likely to occur or has already happened.

THE IMPORTANCE OF CONFIRMATION

In trading the equities markets, one of the biggest mistakes anyone can make is to draw conclusions based on the movement of just one market average. It is not infrequent for one average to reverse direction for weeks or even months, while another average keeps moving in the opposite direction. This is called a divergence and is useful only in a negative sense. As Rhea put it:

Both Averages Must Confirm the movements of both the railroad and industrial stock averages should always be considered together. The movement of one price average must be confirmed by the other before reliable inferences may be drawn. Conclusions based upon the movement of one average, unconfirmed by the other, are almost certain to prove misleading.

Rhea made this observation in 1932. In addition to the Industrial and Railroad (Transportation) indexes, we now have the S&P 500, the Value Line, the Major Market Index, bond indexes, dollar indexes, commodity indexes, and so on. Therefore, bringing this principle up to date implies that instead of "both averages must confirm," the principle should now be "all related averages must confirm." A good example of how this principle must be applied occurred in the period following the October 1987 crash.

First of all, you will recall that one of the "theorems" of Dow Theory is "The theory is not infallible." This was borne out through the crash. Based on Dow Theory, I thought that the crash of October 1987 was the second down leg of a bear market. All related averages went to new lows that broke below previous important lows-a Dow Theory indication of a bear market. But we never entered one. Even so, by a strict Dow Theory reading after the fact, the period following October 19th, 1987, was a secondary correction in a primary bull market, the only one in 91 years that broke below previous secondary lows jointly without leading to a bear market.

It has to be classified as a correction because it did not meet the criterion as defined by Rhea in the definition of a primary bear market. My contention is that if the Fed had not eased in October, and if the Germans and Japanese had not stimulated their economies in December with an infusion of easy credit, a needed bear market would have ensued to correct the malinvestments of previous years. But they did intervene, the S&P bottomed in December, and eventually, the market went to new highs. This is where the principle that "all related averages must confirm' came into play.

First, on April 18, 1989, the Transports broke highs established in August 1987. The Value Line followed on July 10th, followed by the S&P 500 index on July 24 (but only 29% of the group indices within the S&P's went to new highs in 1989). But by a strict Dow Theory reading, the confirmation date didn't occur until April 18, when the Industrials average broke through the August 1987 highs and continued to climb. Now, I classify the period from August 25, 1987, through to December 4, 1987, as a secondary correction in a primary bull market for the Transports, whereas August 25, 1987, to October 19, 1987, is the correction for the Industrials. It was a confusing time, and without the objectivity of Dow Theory to guide investors, it would have been even more confusing.

I should point out that, despite the freak nature of the 1987 market, a rigorous Dow Theory reading gave a clear intermediate sell signal on October 14 when the Dow Industrials broke below the September 21 lows on accelerating volume (the Transports had already made a new low). It didn't matter whether you classified the long-term trend as a bull or a bear. But if you considered the crash the second leg of a bear move, there were no clear long-term buy signals after that.

THE FOUR PHASES OF A MARKET

Two of the key indicators I'm referring to as "signals" is the formation of lines and volume relationships. A market is always in one of four technical phases: (1) It is being accumulated (bought by long-term investors), (2) It is being distributed (sold by long-term investors), (3) It is trending up or down, or (4) It is consolidating (adjusting after profit-taking in a confirmed trend).

Another way to put this is that if a market isn't in a trend, then it is drawing a line. Rhea defined a line as follows:

Lines: -A "line" is a price movement extending two to three weeks or longer, during which period the price variation of both averages moves within a range of approximately 5%. Such an action indicates either accumulation or distribution. Simultaneous advances above the limits of the "line" show accumulation and predict higher prices; conversely, simultaneous declines below the "line" imply distribution, and lower prices are sure to follow. Conclusions are drawn from the movement of one average. Not confirmed by the other, generally prove to be incorrect.

When lines occur, it is usually at intermediate market tops and bottoms, in which case Rhea's definition applies well. At major market tops, prudent long-term investors with superior information try to sell off their (very large) portfolios over a period without creating significant downward pressure on prices. Because there is still enough speculative bullish interest, they manage to distribute their stocks in relatively small lots to traders and speculators. As a result, prices fluctuate up and down without trending up or down over a period of several weeks or more forming a "line." This may also happen on any particular stock and in the commodity markets.

When there is finally a predominance of opinion that prices are going to go down, the line is broken on the downside. In trading terms, this is called "a break "an excellent opportunity to sell short in stocks or commodities

A True Understanding of Trends

At major market bottoms, the same thing often happens, but in reverse. Prudent long-term investors see value after price declines and build up significant positions for their portfolios to hold over the long-term. Whether to test the market or to avoid putting upward pressure on prices, they develop their positions quietly over a period of several weeks to months. The result again is the formation of a line. When there is an interesting aspect of looking for breaks or breakouts is that it is the only time when watching the day to day trend of prices is essential to every market participant, whether trader, speculator or investor. As Rhea put it:

Daily Fluctuations:-Inferences drawn from one day's movement of the averages are almost guaranteed to be misleading and are of but little value except when "lines" are being formed. The day to day movement must be recorded and studied, however, because a series of charted daily changes always eventually develops into a pattern easily recognized as having a forecasting value.

Sometimes, tops and bottoms are reached, and the trend changes without lines being formed. Also, lines sometimes form in the middle of a particular primary trend. This can happen for one of two reasons: either the market has been driven up (or down) rapidly, and many traders and speculators take profits, thus temporarily halting the movement of prices, or the market is uncertain of the future, and the mixture of opinion holds prices at a relatively constant level. In the first case, I call this process consolidation. In the second instance, I call it a waiting market.

IMPORTANT VOLUME RELATIONSHIPS

For trending markets, the volume relationship is significant. As Rhea put it:

The Relation of Volume to Price Movements: -A market which has been overbought becomes dull on rallies and develops activity on declines: conversely, when a market is oversold, the tendency is to become dull on declines and active on rallies. Bull markets terminate in a period of excessive activity and begin with comparatively light transactions.

An "overbought" market is, by definition, one in which prices have been driven up by feelings, hopes, and expectations based on factors other than sound business judgment and value considerations. It occurs at a point after people with superior information have mostly left the market, and general participants are beginning to abandon their former enthusiasm. The market is ripe for a mini panic wherein the slightest sign of a downward move in prices is enough to start a flurry of selling, putting downward pressure on prices. This is why you see relatively high volume on declines and low volume on advances in an overbought market.

Converse reasoning applies to an oversold market. It occurs after a point where shrewd investors have begun to buy securities whose prices have been driven down in a prior sell-off. A resurgence of hopes and expectations builds in the market which, with slight provocation, will grow into a mini-boom in prices on high volume. Although volume relationships apply in any financial market, the stock market is, unfortunately, the only one where volume figures are immediately available. In the commodities markets, estimated volume data are released on the following trading day and the actual numbers two days later. It is important to remember that volume relationship usually, but not always, apply. They should only be used as a subsidiary, not primary, considerations.

CONCLUSION

Now you know what a trend is, what lines are, and some of the key factors which cause or indicate that a trend is changing. You've seen the importance of volume relationships and how they reflect the psychological status of the market. If you learn to think about market behavior in the terms described in this and the last chapter, you will already be a major step ahead of the crowd.

The next step is to reduce this knowledge, especially knowledge of a trend and the change of trend, into a simple and manageable system. What I'm going to present is a charting system that is truly unique and remarkably simple. The system is based on pattern recognition, which is, by definition, a technical method. But before I show it to you, I need to describe both the benefits and the dangers of any technical method.

Chapter 4
The Merits and Hazards of Technical Analysis

Wall Street is full of market technicians. Floor traders, upstairs traders, speculators, and even some long-term investors take advantage of the potential to anticipate market movements by identifying patterns that tend to recur over time. There is no mystery in the reason that these patterns develop. All things being equal, people tend, from a psychological standpoint, to respond to a similar set of conditions in a consistent way. But human psychology is enormously complex, and no two sets of market conditions are ever identical; so technical analysis must be applied cautiously to be used successfully in forecasting market behavior.

According to Robert Edwards and John Magee, "Technical Analysis is the science of recording, usually in graphic form, the actual history of trading (price changes, volume of transactions, and so on) in a certain stock or in 'the averages' and then deducing from that pictured history the probable future trend.'" Their basic premise is very similar to that of Dow Theory-that all of the knowledge available in the marketplace is already factored into prices. But unlike Dow Theory, market technicians think prices and patterns of prices are the only considerations that matter.

I am not a pure technical analyst, but I have made too much money from technical observations to dismiss technical analysis as some "fundamentalists" do. It is an important auxiliary tool which is widely unrecognized by many market players, especially long-term investors, to help make market decisions in which all the odds are in your favor. But standing alone, as the primary means of evaluating an investment or speculative alternatives, technical analysis can not only be ineffective but misleading.

A simple survey of professional traders, speculators, and investors would bear out the degree of efficacy of technical analysis. Those who rely totally on charting methods seldom have consistent records. For example, I was approached by a technical analyst named Tyler who told me that he thought I would profit from his knowledge. I hired him on a trial basis for $500 a week and planned to pay him a percentage of his recommendations that paid out well. Anyway, Tyler was in the office at 6:30 A.M. every day, doing over 120 charts in living color, using methods I still don't understand. He worked 16-hour days, and he obviously knew a lot about the markets, maybe too much for his own good.

When I asked him for recommendations, he would show me the charts and say things like, "This stock might be forming a bottom," or, "This stock looks like it may fill in the gap." But whatever he said, it was always indefinite and always offset by a confusing array of other possibilities. I would ask, "Okay, but what should I do, buy or sell?" Tyler just couldn't give me a simple, straight answer. And what I remember most about him is that the ends of his shirt sleeves were frayed, and his hair always looked unkempt.

I'm not saying that this is the case for all technical analysts, but the point is that technical analysis, as such, does not lend itself to thinking in essentials. If you watch any financial news, and you should, you'll see what I'm talking about. Different technical analysts interpret patterns differently, and they all have their own story. In my view, the best thing to do is identify just a few essential technical principles and use them as auxiliary tools. Those who encompass these kinds of technical methods into a broader system which includes rigorous and sound analysis of economic fundamentals and detailed evaluation of specific securities and commodities do quite well by them.

For purposes of this discussion, it is important to understand the activities of three major groups of technicians: tide watchers, manipulators, and purists.

TIDE WATCHERS

Tide watchers are what I call those who attempt to buy and sell in the direction of the intraday ebbs and surges of price trends. This group is relatively unconcerned with the state of the economy, the price-earnings ratio or earnings growth of a given stock, or any other underlying market fundamentals. Rather, their focus is almost entirely on the direction of price movements from moment to moment and day today. The market moves up or down or sideways, and their goal is to be buyers or sellers or flat accordingly.

Tide watchers are the locals in the pits of the futures exchanges, the market makers, and the floor traders on any of the major exchanges. They fit into the category of technicians because their sole interest is in the price trend-"The trend is your friend" is the essence of their thinking. Typically, instead of any significant news, they try to ride the trend while watching "resistance" and "support" points previous highs or lows that make other tidal-type participants wary.

In an uptrend, a previous high point above the current price level is resistance; whereas a previous low supports. In a downtrend, a previous low point below the current price is resistance, whereas a previous high supports. In an uptrend, if a previous high is broken and prices continue to climb, then the tide watchers are buyers, and any significant succession of down ticks is a possible sell signal. If a previous high is broken and prices fail to move further upward, they are sellers, and any significant upward movement is a possible buy signal. Converse reasoning applies to significant low points. Tide watchers always try to be attuned to what the ever present "They" are thinking and what "They" will do next, and their method of measurement is the character of changing price movements.

Since tide watchers make up the bulk of the floor traders on the exchanges, it is in the best interest of the speculator and investor to be aware of their potential impact on the short term price trend. They can quickly drive the price of a particular stock or commodity up or down several points in the near future, with nothing but their interactions creating the movement.

For example, suppose that floor traders on a stock exchange observe that offerings for XYZ are light and that declining prices don't result in any significant liquidation. If this pattern continues, they might conclude quite reasonably that there is very little interest to sell XYZ. The logical thing for them to do is pick up

The Merits and Hazards of Technical Analysis

the stock at any sign of weakness-to buy the stock at what they perceive as short-term bargain prices-and test the market.

Suppose that XYZ is 40 1/4 bid, offered at 40 1/3 For simplicity, assume that only 500 shares of the stock are offered at N. The floor traders can only guess how much is available at Y2, and so on; but thinking that long interest is strong, some shrewd fellow on the floor decides to test the market by buying the stock and waiting to see what the change, if any, in buying and selling interest will be. In particular, he watches to see if any outside orders come in as a result of the price change, and if so, whether they are buy or sell orders.

If sell orders come in, then the trader rids himself of the stock and tries another day again. But if a few buy orders come in and are filled at perhaps y2, then a few more brokers join in. If the process continues, then very quickly a short-term bullish atmosphere is created for the stock.

Up to this point, the floor trader has no idea whether or not there was any change in the earnings prospects for XYZ company, although it is likely that there is some reason for the initial lack of interest to sell. But regardless of the company's prospects, if the movement gains a large enough following on the floor, a miniboom in the price of the stock can occur. After all, the bullish floor traders involved all have an interest in the price going up.

On the other hand, large sell orders coming from outside can, at any point, squelch the rally. And like any pyramid scheme, to the extent that the mini-boom is purely speculative, those participants at the top stand to lose the most. Similar reasoning is applied to a mini-bust, which quite commonly occurs shortly after the mini-boom. Program trading can initiate, accelerate, and amplify the whole process.

Speculators or investors who are aware of the effects of tide watcher-type activity can use their knowledge in several ways. First, practiced "upstairs'" observers can recognize this kind of activity on their monitors and optimize profits by careful timing of their intermediate-term, and long-term buys and sells within the intraday cycle. Second, the "legitimacy" of price changes, regarding their intermediate-term and long-term, staying power, can be gauged according to the relationship of the price move to market fundamentals and the movement of the markets considered as a whole. And finally, the character of tide watcher's activity can be a key indicator of the consensus on the Street.

This last point is probably the most important for the speculator. Like geologists who attempt to predict volcanic activity or earthquakes by monitoring seismic activity, speculators can gauge the tremors of coming market events by monitoring intraday and day to day activity. Specifically, volume numbers, the ratio of advancing issues to declining issues, the short-term response to important economic or market news, and the rate of change of prices all can contribute to an estimate of the predominant driving psychology of market participants.

In the case of the October 13, 1989, sell-off in the stock market, the news that financing fell through on the United Airlines takeover sent the market into a selling panic. This was a clear indication that the tenor of the market was wary. The market opinion was skeptical about the strength of the ongoing bull market-one more sign to indicate that a bear, or at least a secondary correction, might be near at hand.

THE MANIPULATORS

Manipulation is a dirty word on Wall Street. It carries a connotation of the kind of unfairness and dishonesty associated with a fixed horse race or dealing from the bottom of the deck in a card game. But in fact, it is an entirely different thing. According to the Random House Dictionary, to manipulate is to "manage or influence by artful skill." Webster's Collegiate Edition adds a secondary meaning "to control or play upon by artful, unfair, or insidious means." But there is nothing manifestly "insidious" or "unfair" about attempting to profit by managing one's buying and selling activity to cause a change in a price and profit by the move-that is unless the SEC (Securities and Exchange Commission) thinks there is. Then it becomes insidious because you can go to jail for it. Individuals go to jail, but institutions don't.

The large institutional houses use massive buy and sell programs to Manipulate market prices in the short term. Their objective is to profit by playing the disparities in prices between related markets, variations often induced or exaggerated by their activity. They rely on the psychology of the tide watchers for their success.

Suppose for example that a $2 billion pension fund decides to liquidate $100 million of its stock portfolio. Knowing that the sale of such large blocks of stocks will probably send the market indexes lower, it decides to take advantage of the fact. During a typically quiet period, usually around 2 PM., it begins to sell S&P Index futures to consolidate a $200 million short position. This is double the amount of the cash stock position and would take somewhere in the neighborhood of 1,000 to 1,500 contracts to attain-a number easily accommodated by the S&P futures market.

Then, at about 3:10 PM., the institution begins scale selling of stocks to the tune of about $10 million worth of stocks every five minutes or so, finishing off with one large block sale at the close. Because of the enormous amounts of money and stock traded, short interest is generated on the floor of the stock exchange, and prices begin moving down. In response, the price of the futures moves down proportionally. Tide watchers ride the crest and accelerate the move in both the cash and the futures markets into a mini-bust.

The institution, while losing a little money by selling stocks on the way down, is more than compensated by the gain made in buying back a successful (and double-sized) short position in futures on the way down. Bear in mind that the margin requirement for the futures is 5%, whereas the margin requirement for stocks is 50%; so using leverage, the upside profit potential is ten times greater in the futures market.

The next morning, the tide reverses, and buying interest builds, creating a mini-boom. By knowing in advance-with solid certainty-the results of its massive involvement, the institution can time its buys and sells and make a handsome profit for itself and its clients in both markets and both directions, plus generate some nice commission or fee business. In the end, the market is effectively unchanged, but a lot of money has changed hands. There are many different types of programs, some of them incredibly complex, and not all of them are manipulative. But all in all, it's an excellent racket.

For the sake of justice, it should be noted that any "unfairness" inherent in program trading is due not to the practice itself, but to the government's arbitrary regulation of the markets. If "manipulation" is condemned when practiced by an individual but tolerated if done on a camouflaged but massive scale by institutions, that is unfair. As William J. O'Neil put it:

They [the institutions] are allowed to hook up directly to the New York Stock Exchange's computers and spit out massive market orders instantaneously. You and I must contact our brokers and have them transmit our orders by wire to New York, for execution several minutes later.

Instead of complete deregulation of the markets, which is the ideal alternative as far as I'm concerned, the least the regulators could do is define clearly what "manipulation" is so that everyone understands the requirements of trading within the bounds of so-called "legality."

Beginning in the mid-1980s, programs completely changed the character of intraday price movements, introducing a degree of uncertainty that never existed before. Now, at any moment, the judgment of one program manager can start a buy or sell program that may create a swing in the market of from 5 to 30 or more points on a purely technical basis.

One used to day-trade the S&P futures by the clock. Before programs, you never saw a sell-off last more than one or two hours without some rally. You also very rarely saw the kind of spikes in either direction as you see them now. Because the institutions deal in such massive size, and because the public has fled the markets when you day-trade the S&Ps now, it feels like you are performing with a gun on your back. At any moment, a program manager can pull the trigger, and the market roars against you before you have time to get out with just a small loss, especially if you are trading large size.

Being caught on the wrong side of a program-induced swing in the short term can be deadly financially to the trader or speculator. But being on the right side can be equally rewarding. The problem is that since one person's judgment causes the move, and since no one knows the plan but that person and perhaps a handful of others, being involved in short-term trading is much more difficult today and often can turn into something of a crapshoot. However, by watching the charts of the S&P 500 cash and S&P 500 futures index, prudent speculators or investors can learn to recognize the pattern of program price movements and time their buys and sells to optimize profits.' This kind of market timing can add significantly to portfolio profits. Conversely, to buy or sell large blocks of stocks or futures "at the market" in the presence of a program is simply foolish.

Over the intermediate-term and long-term, programs cannot fundamentally manipulate prices, but they can change the character of the price trend, accelerating intermediate price movements in one direction or the other. On the upside, their massive involvement can generate long speculative interest. On the short side, they can have a devastating impact on the speed of significant market downturns, as happened in the October 1987 crash. Coming into October, the market was in trouble from a fundamental point of view. Prices were at 21 times earnings, one of the highest PEs in history.

The average book value to price ratio was nominally greater than it was in 1929, and if adjusted for inflation, was much greater. These factors, especially when combined with record-breaking debt figures at all levels, made the market ripe for, at a minimum, a significant correction. The question at the time was not "if" but "when."

The billions of dollars of institutional money involved in the markets before October 19 was there purely to profit through the various short-term hedge, arbitrage, and manipulative strategies. It was evident that if the Fed tightened substantially, or if the dollar fell significantly, this "hot" money would be withdrawn from the market, dramatically accelerating the downward move.

THE PURISTS

Some technical analysts believe, on a formal, theoretical basis, that price is everything, that everything known or knowable concerning the future of the markets is already contained in market prices and their movements. These are the technical purists, notably R. N. Elliot, Krondodiov, and on a more limited scale, some unthinking followers of the teachings of Edwards and Magee, and some heretical Dow Theorists. In variant forms and to various extents, the technical purists presume that there is an inevitability to price movements, that they are somehow determined by some universal force, and that economic analysis and forecasting consists of finding the right mathematical correlations or cycle times to characterize the movements.

Any attempt to forecast the future by rigorous cycle theory or by strictly mathematical means ignores the subjective nature of the market activity. Also, such efforts ignore the fact that government intervention and Federal Reserve policy can dramatically influence the long-term trend, as will be shown in later chapters. To the extent that individuals are successful in applying these types of theoretical systems to market forecasting and analysis, it is because they depart from the rigor that consistency would require. Either their formulations temporarily characterize market behavior because of the consistent behavior of market participants, in which case it is merely a short-term technical observation, or the formulations themselves are so general and so loosely defined that they permit interpretation and individual reasoning to be imposed on them.

In the first case, basing speculative or investment decisions on technical models which predict in advance extent and duration points will be inconsistent-market conditions can change rapidly. In the second case, the formulations are little more than an obstacle to sound reasoning and analysis. In both instances, inevitably, conditions will change, attitudes will change, and their market models fall flat.

Again, I want to emphasize that I am not speaking here of all methods and applications of technical analysis, just those that claim that the future is predetermined and therefore predictable with rigorous mathematical models.

SUMMARY

Technical analysis provides vital information as long as it is recognized for what it is: a method of characterizing recurring patterns of price movements. These patterns result from a predominantly similar psychological tendency of market participants in making decisions. The greatest value of technical analysis is that it provides a method for measuring the tendency of the market to react in a particular way under similar conditions throughout history.

Given this recognition, technical analysis adds a valuable dimension to market analysis and economic forecasting that is often overlooked by speculators and investors. If understood and concretely defined, technical observations add to the sum of one's knowledge about the nature of the markets and provide an opportunity to identify profitable opportunities that would otherwise go unseen.

Chapter 5
What the Analysts Don't Know Can Kill You

HOW IMPORTANT CAN ANCHOVIES BE?

I often marvel at the sophistication of the reports that analysts put out-so much detailed research, such complex determinations of "market value." Invariably, analysts' reports contain all kinds of interesting information, and the best of them are well-reasoned, well-written, and entirely convincing. But do you know what? I haven't read one in years.

When I give talks to groups of market professionals, I sometimes open up by asking the following question: "If the tide shifts out off the coast of Peru, would you be a buyer or a seller of soybeans?

Usually. I get looks that say. "I thought this guy was good at what he does. What the hell is he talking about'?"

Then I explain that when the tide shifts outward, the anchovies that feed in the shallows off the coast of Peru move further out into the Pacific. The anchovy fishermen whose primary market is the Japanese who feed anchovies to cattle lose yield. The supply of anchovies dry up and the Japanese start feeding their animals with soybean products. The demand for soybeans goes up, and so does the price of soybean and soy meal futures. Therefore, if the tide shifts out off the coast of Peru, you should be a buyer of soybeans.

At this point. I've usually captured the attention of most of the audience, but there are still a lot of looks out there that say, "So what" The point of the story is not that you should find a way to monitor the tides off the coast of Peru to trade soybeans efficiently. The point is that you don't have to know everything there is to be known about a market to trade it. In fact, there is no way you can know everything, and it will probably be the one thing you don't know or haven't thought about that will burn you if you try to trade from knowledge of the specifics of a market. In other words, what the analysts don't know can kill you.

Like Peter Lynch explained in his book One Up on Wall Street, common sense is usually more useful than a myriad of facts and figures. But where Lynch and I differ is in my conviction that if you know what to look for the market will tell you most of what you need to know. In particular, there are a few key technical indicators that are right more often than not and have stood the test of time throughout my entire career.

In glancing through my copy of Technical Analysis of Stock Trends, by Edwards and Magee, I counted over 20 different technical patterns discussed in just five chapters. With all due respect to Edwards and Magee and their elegant and useful book, I do not recommend using most of these complex technical observations as a primary tool in trading. A few technical tools, however, are of tremendous value as secondary measures of the merits or pitfalls of any trade, especially in the stock market. I call these technical tools "secondary" because I never base any trading decision on them alone. I use them more to tell me what not to do than what to do.

The secondary technical tools that I use most are:

1. Moving averages

2. Relative strength indicators

3. Momentum indicators (oscillators)

As I have said before, the art of speculation consists of putting money at risk only when the odds are in your favor. These secondary technical observations serve to supplement odds measurement. Of all the technical measures that I know about, other than those discussed in the last chapter, these work the best.

UNDERSTANDING MOVING AVERAGES

A moving average is simply an average of successive numbers over a specified period which is constantly updated by dropping the oldest number in succession, adding the newest number, and then totaling and averaging.

For example, to obtain the 10-day moving average of the daily closing of the Dow Jones Industrials, you start by summing and averaging ten consecutive days. On the eleventh day, you add that closing number to the previous 10-day sum. Then subtract the first day, and divide by 10 to get the updated average. By continuing this process on a daily basis, the average "moves" from day to day: that is it changes in a way that takes into account the latest closing price.

What's the point of doing this? Moving averages tend to smooth out erratic fluctuations in market price movements, and they are useful in determining trends and trend reversals. Because they are averages over a specified period they are by definition, dampened indices which lag behind more immediate price fluctuations. The longer the averaging period you use, the greater is the dampening or lag. Effect. By studying various moving averages, it is possible to identify certain repeating patterns which can be used to determine the probable course of the price trend. Some of the patterns are so well-defined that they can be used as buy or sell signals in both stocks and commodities.

Virtually every stock chart book that I have ever seen uses some moving average. Many individual technicians and traders use their own moving average formulations, weighting the near weeks or using exponentials in their calculations. But rather than discuss the variety and type available, let me tell you which ones I use and how I use them.

As far as I'm concerned, in the equities markets (individual stocks and stock indexes), by far the most useful of all the moving averages I've seen is the 200-day (that's 200-trading day or 40-week) moving average.

I keyed into this in college when I read the results of a study by William Gordon demonstrating that by buying and selling the Dow Jones Industrials stocks from 1917 to 1967 using only the 200-day moving average, an investor could have realized an average yearly simple return of 18.5%. By comparison, his study showed that Dow Theory would have achieved 18.1% per year if an investor bought and sold on confirmation days of bull and bear markets.' In the study, Gordon used two simple rules to determine buy and sell signals from the moving average:

1. If the 200-day moving average line flattens out following a previous decline or is advancing, and prices penetrate the moving average line on the upside, this comprises a major buying signal.

2. If the 200-day moving average line flattens out following a previous rise or is declining, and prices penetrate the moving average line on the downside, this comprises a major selling signal.

You can use the long-term moving average as a predictor not only for the averages but also on individual stocks and most commodity futures. I use it for two basic purposes-to confirm Dow Theory in determining the course of the long-term trend and in making specific stock selections.

When picking stocks, I never buy a stock when prices are below the moving average, and I never sell a stock when the price is above the moving average. Just pick up any chart book that uses a 35 or 40-week moving average, and you'll see why the odds of being right are way against you.

As far as using other, shorter-term, moving averages. I have only found one other set of observation that works consistently and stands the test of time. This works not only for stocks and stock indexes but for many commodities as well.

Of course, as with all technical observations, these observations are never right 100% of the time. For example, you would have been destroyed on October 19. 1987 if you used only the 10-

week/30-week cross rule. By the time you got the sell signal, the crash was over.

For the commodity futures markets, there is no hard and fast rule about which long-term moving average works best it varies from market to market and over time. For example, at this writing, the 200-day works well for bonds, the dollar index, and gold but not so well for the other commodities.

You've got to recognize that, as a technical tool, the validity of the moving averages is apt to change with changing market conditions. The shorter the term that you trade in, the more this is true. So, you have to experiment with different times and find the ones that work. When they quit working, you've got to change again. For example, on pork bellies, I've been using the 4-week and 11-week moving averages, and I apply a rule similar to the 10-week/30-week rule I described above. Just recently, however, the relationship has started to get sloppy, so it might be time to experiment with the time periods again.

The biggest mistake anyone can make in using moving averages, or any technical observation for that matter is to fall in love with it. By that I mean don't ever think you have found "the rule to end all rules"; no such thing exists. Every market is in a constant process of change, and any method which doesn't take change into account in a fundamental way is subject to being wrong.

In philosophy, I strongly disagree with the school of Pragmatism,- but when it comes to trading rules, you have to be entirely pragmatic. A rule is right only as long as it works. When it quits working, you've got to kiss it goodbye and leave it alone. Otherwise, just like a bad relationship with a person, it will bring you down. I've seen it happen to individuals who were at one time considered to be among the best traders on Wall Street. So be careful not to get emotionally involved with any discovery you make when identifying patterns using the moving averages or any technical method.

A DIFFERENT PERSPECTIVE ON RELATIVE STRENGTH

To the best of my knowledge, the concept of relative strength was first discussed by Robert Rhea in a Baryon's article in 1933. He didn't call it relative strength but rather the "habits of stocks and how they perform against one another." Relative strength is simply a ratio between a single stock against a stock group or an average index, or between a stock group and a larger group or average index.

Like moving averages, there are all kinds of different formulations of relative strength. Some chart books, for example, weight recent weeks more heavily than others. For example, in New York Stock Exchange Daily Graphs, each stock has a relative strength line which is a plot of the ratio of the stock price to the S&P 500 Index on a weekly basis, plus there is another time-weighted relative strength indicator which compares the percentage change of the stocks price to the change in price of stocks in the database. The number varies from 1 to 99. The number 52, for example, would indicate that the stock outperformed 52% of all other stocks in the database. The idea of relative strength is sometimes difficult to understand because we are brought up with a consumer mentality. As kids, we watch our parents look for sales, and most of us carry on that tradition; we all try to buy cheap and sell high.

For example, assuming that you like citrus fruit, if you went to the grocery store and saw that both oranges and grapefruit were selling at fifty cents per pound, you would probably buy a few of each. But if you went back a week later and found grapefruit suddenly at a dollar per pound and oranges still at fifty cents, you would probably opt just to buy oranges and wait for a better market in grapefruit. If you use this same kind of thinking in buying stocks, you are often making a terrible mistake.

You should never buy a stock simply because it's cheap; the chances are that it is probably cheap for a good reason. What you want is a stock that is going to perform, that is going to appreciate in value faster than the average stock. Relative strength is a measure of this kind of performance. All things being equal, if you are looking to buy a stock, you should buy the strongest performers, as indicated by the best measurement of relative strength available.

So far, I've discussed how relative strength is typically used. There is another way of looking at the relative strength that relates directly to my definition of a trend. Recall that when the market is in an uptrend, it makes a series of higher lows and higher highs. So, what I do is look at the Industrials average, and if it has made a higher high, then I look for stocks that have made a higher high on the same day as, or on days before the average.

These are the strongest stocks-the market leaders. If the market is in an uptrend, then these are the stocks that, everything else being equal, you would want to buy, but not when they make the higher highs. You buy them on reactions, during sell-offs, because the chances for fast returns are better. Strong relative strength stocks move more quickly on the upside than the other stocks in the market.

When playing the short side near market tops, I don't recommend shorting strong relative strength stocks, because if you are wrong, then you will lose more money. Nor do I recommend shorting the weakest stocks, because they often don't have far to move on the downside. I prefer to short the mid-range relative strength stocks because if you are wrong, you don't get hurt too badly, and if you are right, you can still make some hefty profits.

The time to short the strong stocks is after an intermediate-term, or long-term top has occurred in both the Industrials and the Transports, and you get a confirmed change of trend in the stock by the 1-2-3 criterion. This kind of action is ideal for picking up some quick profits in the short term because if the market continues to sell off after you get a confirmed top in a strong stock, the stock's price is liable to fall continuously for one to three days in what is effectively a panic move. It is best to take profits quickly on this kind of trade, however, because there will be plenty of buyers looking for a bargain in the stock because of its previous strength, and the price is apt to recover quickly.

While relative strength is an important secondary indicator, I place it lower on the scale of importance than moving averages. In other words, if the stock price is below the moving average and the relative strength is good, I weight the moving average more heavily and pass the stock up as a potential buy.

The concept of relative strength is applicable in the commodities markets as well, but the way you apply it is slightly different. If you are considering a long position in the precious metals, for instance, you would compare the relative strength of gold, silver, platinum, etc., to one another and buy the strongest of the group. For example, Figure 8.8 shows the weekly bar charts of gold and silver. You can also use relative strength in the commodities to determine how to position yourself in a hedge or spread. When looking at the grains, for example, compare the relative strength of corn to wheat.

Moving objects have a property called momentum, which is what you might call the quantity of motion of an object. The actual measurement of momentum is the product of something's mass times its velocity. A swinging pendulum, for example, has constantly changing momentum.

Although not in the strict physical sense, markets also have momentum. You can think of the plot of the pendulum's momentum as idealized market behavior, where prices oscillate around a steady center point, where the velocity of price changes is constantly changing and the reverses at the top and bottom of the plot corresponding to market tops and bottoms.

But unlike a pendulum, which has a constant mass and changing velocity, market momentum has both constantly evolving mass and constantly changing speed. In addition, there are forces which influence the market, such as breaking major political or economic news, that can radically shift market momentum at any time.

Consequently, it is impossible to measure market momentum with complete accuracy and use the measurement to predict market turning points with certainty. It is possible, however, to develop correlations that closely approximate market momentum and help predict when the price trend is changing. The best of these indicators are called oscillators.

To the best of my knowledge, the term oscillators, which is now a standard industry term, was initially used by H. M. Gartley in his book, Profits in the Stock Market, first published in 1935. Like moving averages and relative strength indexes, oscillators come in a variety of formulations, but the element common to them all is that they measure the differences in some market parameter over some particular period. They are, therefore, measurements of the rate of change of some important market parameter such as price, breadth, moving averages, or volume; and they oscillate around a baseline, much like the plot of the momentum of the pendulum.

For the equities markets, I use two oscillators-one for the breadth and one for the price. For commodities, I use an oscillator based upon the difference between two moving averages. The oscillators I use for the stock indexes, price and breadth, have remained valid since I first started using them in January 2003. The one I use for commodities is built into my quote system, and you can change the period of the moving averages until you find "a good fit" for the particular product you are dealing with. Referring to the figures, you can see that a good oscillator begins reversing when or before the market trend starts to change. In most cases, these particular oscillators are quite accurate. Typically, when the market is in an uptrend. I did use two price oscillators for the Industrials, one short-term and one long-term, but the advent of program trading in the mid-80s invalidated the more near-term oscillator.

The oscillator will also be moving up. The higher the oscillator rises on the chart, the more the market approaches an "overbought" condition. Ideally, just like the plot of the pendulum, as the market approaches the top, the oscillator will "slow down," that is, flatten out and top. Then, as prices start to reverse, the oscillator will turn down and continue down until the market approaches an "oversold" condition when the reverse of what happens at a top occurs.

Generally speaking, the higher or lower the oscillator lines go above or below the baseline relative to other peaks and valleys in the plot, the more significant they become. Now let me show you how to calculate the precise oscillators that I use and demonstrate exactly how I use them.

The best momentum measurement I use for stock market breadth is really what you might call a 10-day equivalent, net change, moving average, breadth oscillator. It sounds complicated, but it is quite simple. Before I get into it, however, let me say a few words about breadth.

Breadth is an indicator used to counterbalance the fact that most stock average indices are weighted. The Dow Industrials, for example, is an average of only 30 stocks weighted to price. Sometimes, if a heavily weighted stock makes an unusually large move, it can throw the average off as a good indicator of general industrial stock performance. One way to test the validity of the averages as general market indicators is to compare them to what is called the advance/decline line, that is, breadth.

The A/D line is simply a plot of the difference between the total number of advancing issues and the total number of declining issues of every stock on the New York Stock Exchange versus time in days. The A/D line moves with the Dow, and when there is a divergence between them, it often signals a coming change in the trend.

The breadth oscillator is simply a measure of market momentum, and it often gives you an earlier signal of a coming change in trend than does the A/D line by itself.

I use two breadth oscillators, one short term, and one long term, but I pay much more attention to the longer term one. For the short term, every morning, first I log the net A/D number; I simply calculate, log, and plot a moving sum of advancing issues minus declining issues on the NYFE for the previous ten days. In other words, every day, I keep a running, cumulative total of the daily difference of advancing issues minus declining issues.

A quick comparison of the breadth momentum lines to the daily closing prices of the Industrials shows a good correlation between turns in the oscillators and intermediate price reversals on the Dow. You will note, however, that if you traded by turns in the short-term oscillator, you would get "whipped out" on several occasions. The long-term oscillator, on the other hand, sometimes lags changes in intermediate trend, such that trading by it alone would cost you money. That's why I use them as supporting tools. But overall, the correlation is excellent and has been since I first began using it in 2003

The price oscillator I use is slightly more complex, and it is also more important regarding the weight I place on it in evaluating the market. Again every morning, using the daily closing prices on the New York Composite Index, I begin by calculating the difference between the previous day's closing price and the closing price from the last fifth day. Then, I add the result to the sum of the same result for the previous nine trading days, to give a 10-day running sum of the five-day price difference. A plot of the daily result compared to the Industrials average shows a highly significant correlation between turns in the oscillator and turns in the daily closing prices of the stock index.

I use the breadth and price oscillators to anticipate coming market turning points and to confirm them when they occur. A simple look at the charts will show that the higher or lower the oscillator goes on the chart, the greater is the chance of an intermediate change of trend. Like a warning light on railroad tracks, when the oscillators approach or break through significant previous highs or lows, they are telling you that danger is ahead. They don't speak the nature of the danger, or how far ahead it lies, but they do tell you to proceed with caution or continue full speed ahead.

For commodities, as I have already mentioned, my quote system has an oscillator measurement built-in to it which is the difference between two moving averages. The nice thing about this feature is that it allows you to readily change and experiment with different time periods for the moving averages until you find one that fits the movement of the particular market you are trading.

This is essential in the commodity markets because, any time you are dealing with one item versus an average, the chances of conditions arising which change the nature of "normal" price behavior are much greater. Oscillators in the commodity markets are, therefore, much less reliable than they are for the stock average indices. Nevertheless, if you find the right one, they can be of tremendous value in confirming trend changes.

In fact, sometimes you can get a correlation that is so good that you could virtually make your trading decisions on them alone and make quite a bit of money. I never do this, nor do I recommend it, but it is possible, and I'm sure many traders do it. The problem with this approach is that when you are wrong, you will often be wrong in a huge way.

Many technicians get very sophisticated with oscillators and use them, not just for the averages, but for specific stocks as well.

I don't.

There is such a thing as acquiring too much information. I think you are better off using a few oscillators at most, and then only as secondary measures to affirm or deny the first change of trend indicators I discussed in the last chapter.

MAKING STOCK SELECTIONS

So far, all of the methods I've discussed apply to virtually any market, from specific stocks to commodities, to indexes. Undoubtedly, some of you trade only individual stocks-something I used to put my primary focus on. For making stock selections, so far we have Dow Theory to make a general market call and, within that context, the technical methods I've described to pick out a group of stocks that are likely to move with or against the market. Now, we'll cover a few auxiliary methods which will help you select specific stocks. The objective, of course, is to put even more of the odds in your favor.

The Technical versus the Fundamental Approach

There is a whole group of traders, some independent, some working for firms, called stock pickers-people who choose stocks for trading, speculating, or investing. Within this group, there are two primary schools of thought-the purely technical school and the purely fundamental school. My experience has been that it is a very rare purist who consistently makes money.

Most profitable stock speculators are hybrids; they combine the best of both worlds and use a combination of technical and fundamental tools. I would have to call myself a hybrid who leans toward the technical side. I combine the technical methods described in the last chapter, which is likely to reflect the future judgment of market participants, with vital statistics which consistently correlate to price movements over time.

The fundamentalists believe that, over the long term, the market prices stocks according to yield, earning power, and the value of each company's underlying assets. In other words, the value is determined by those three intrinsic factors for any stock. The problem I have with this approach is that it ignores the subjective nature of value; it doesn't take into account that people, not computers, ultimately determine the price. For the fundamentalist view to be accurate, yield, earning power, and assets would have to reflect the collective judgment of the market place directly. They don't. In fact, fundamentalists are notorious for being "right." but with bad timing.

One very modern fundamentalist offshoot is the Graham and Dodd approach to stock selection. Highly oversimplified, the Graham and Dodd approach says that you should buy low PE (price/earnings ratio), low book value stocks. The underlying premise is that these are likely to be the "undervalued" growth stocks, whereas the higher PE stocks have already been recognized and properly "evaluated" by the market. As long as you are in the early to late-middle stages of an inflationary bull market, this approach works pretty well stock prices for all, but the worst of companies appreciate. But over time, it can get you in trouble. Usually, when a stock has a low PE and a low book value, there are reasons for it, and the market already knows those reasons.

I find PEs and book value very useful but in a different way. If you look at PEs and book value of the indexes as a whole and compare them to historical PEs and book values, you find a good secondary indicator of overbought and oversold conditions of the averages as a whole. Then, you can compare the individual stocks PE and book value to those of the averages, and gauge, again as a secondary indicator, the relative performance of the specific stock to the market regarding an overbought or oversold condition.

Rate of Change of Earnings Growth

One fundamental statistic that is excellent is the correlation between the rate of change of earnings growth and the change in the stock price. In a book published in 1969, Gordon Holmes demonstrated that "The slope of a given price trend almost always precedes the correspondent or equivalent earnings trend slope in time. The amount of time displacement is about three months."

There are three things I like about this observation. First, it is usually true. Second, it has withstood the test of time. And third, it supports the fundamental precept of Dow Theory that the markets "discount everything." Now, how do you use this observation?

First of all, you have to establish that the correlation holds true for the stock you are evaluating. Most businesses have seasonal fluctuations which cause variations in earnings, so you should look at earnings figures for no less than six quarters before considering earnings growth as a valid indicator of future price changes. A plot of the earnings curve on the same time base should give you a direct correlation between earnings growth and price growth. The relationship should exist for the entire period considered; otherwise, this indicator should be disregarded entirely for that stock.

Holmes developed a rather complicated method for stock picks based on earnings growth and other factors; I use earnings growth a little bit differently. In William O'Neil's New York Stock Exchange Daily Graphs, earnings are reported in quarters, with the next quarter's projected earnings included. If the correlation holds, then on the bull side, if the rate of change of earnings growth is less than the rate of change of prices, then the stock is a buy. If the rate of change in earnings growth is equal to or greater than the price trend slope, then look for a better stock. The reverse holds true on the bear side.

If you trade a stock on this basis, with other technical reasons included, I want to warn you about something: so many people trade on earnings that estimated quarterly earnings reports could kill you, particularly on high PE stocks-they sometimes crash very fast. Find out when the actual earnings figures come out, and if the stock is near its highs, get out before the reports come out. If they come out less than expected, the stock can easily gap down, and your accumulated profits will disappear!

The whole idea of looking at yield and PEs is to identify stocks with high growth potential. However, rate of change of earnings growth is the primary number to check for finding growth stocks. Yield, for example, is dividend divided by price. Naturally, a high yield can result from a high dividend being paid by a company with a depressed stock price. But why is the price low? Because the earnings are lousy!

Both Citicorp and Traveler's had declining prices but increasing yields for six months or so as of July 1990. The companies have kept up their dividend payment while the stock price has been falling. Since the stock prices have fallen in greater proportion than earnings, the PEs of both stocks have also fallen. What you have in this situation is two stocks with low PEs and high yields. Does that make them a good buy?

I don't think so. What if both companies continue to perform poorly? PEs and yield can be very misleading, if not viewed in the context of earnings growth. I often think regarding the phrase, "Wherever a stock price goes, there it is!" It is a good reminder that it is highly unlikely that you will spot an underpriced stock before the rest of the market.

Let me give you an example which illustrates why earnings growth is such an important aspect of picking stocks. Eighty percent of all companies listed on the NYSE pay out 30 to 65% of their revenues in dividends-those that earn money. Assume the stock of a young company is selling at $10 per share, is currently earning $1 per share, is paying a $.50 dividend (50% of earnings and a 5% yield), and has a rate of earnings growth of 25%. Both the PE of 10 and the yield of 5% are mid-range and say little about the stock as a buy. But the 25% rate of earnings growth tells a lot more!

With a 25% growth rate, the company's earnings will double in 2.9 years. Assuming the same percentage dividend payment, if you buy the stock now, your yield will double in roughly three years, and double again three years after that. If the stock continues in its rate of earnings growth, you will pay out your investment, in dividends alone, in less than eight years, not to mention the equity appreciation you would most likely enjoy. Picking stocks based on yield and PEs alone will tell you nothing about this kind of potential.

There are a few other fundamental considerations which I use to make a final decision if, on balance, everything else is equal in choosing between two stocks.

First, given two similar bullish charts, I would pick the lower PE stock as a buy. Conversely, if both charts were equally bearish, I would pick the higher PE stock as a short.

Second, in a buy, I would always choose to buy the stock of a company in a less leveraged position over a company in a more leveraged position; the greater the leverage, the greater the susceptibility to a credit crunch. The converse is true in a sell. Third, whether buying or selling, I always trade the stock with the most shares on the market to ensure liquidity.

As a final consideration concerning the fundamental approach, part of being a speculator in the stock market is being able to judge whether or not a new product or service offered by a new or established company will be accepted favorably by the market. In these kinds of cases, the traders in the stock markets are sometimes wrong, and either fail to anticipate consumer demand for a great new product or over-anticipate a new product that bombs.

I don't very often participate in these kinds of speculations, but they are speculations nonetheless. The reason I don't is that there is no way to measure the odds. This is where I think simple common sense comes into play. If a new product is great, tastes good, is unique, is well marketed-if you believe it is going to take off big for common sense reasons then by all means, buy some stock if you can afford to lose your investment.

A Few Extra Words about Technical Methods

Aside from the technical tools in this and the last chapter, there is one more thing I want to add about the technical evaluation of stock charts. All of the tenets of Dow Theory apply to individual stocks; they just aren't quite as valid.

In any statistical study, the more samples you have, the more repeatable the results are likely to be. A single stock has many of the characteristics of a market average index. For example, the sum of all knowledge about that stock is expressed in the movement of the price. Volume relationships are much the same. The psychology of the stock cycle is much the same. Most things are the same. But the first premise of Dow Theory is that it is not infallible. The same is true for individual stocks, only more so. Also, you have to draw all inferences for individual stocks without the benefit of another index for confirmation. Nevertheless, it is useful to apply Dow Theory's technical observations to individual stocks.

CONCLUSION

At this point, you are equipped with a simple but powerful set of technical tools with which to approach the analysis of price movements in the financial markets. We move from the general principles and concepts of Dow Theory to primary technical considerations, to secondary technical factors, to some more particularized technical and fundamental considerations for individual stocks. In the next chapters, we will add some powerful, common sense, fundamental economic considerations to our speculating arsenal.

Chapter 6
The Science of Madness

THE PUZZLE BOX

Imagine trying to solve a puzzle box that has no patterns or instructions. Assume that all the sides were the same shade of gray, and each side was cut in a similar pattern with only slight variations. The process of solving the puzzle would not only be unendurably tedious, but the only result would be a meaningless gray smear in the shape of a cube. Do you think you would seriously attempt to solve such a puzzle? I doubt it. Although you may question the motivation of the designer, you would probably shrug it off leaving it to those eccentric few that could find some obscure purpose in its solution.

Most people view contemporary economics like the hypothetical puzzle box -tedious and unrewarding-and economists as characters looking for a solution to an unendurably complex problem. It is hard to understand the relationship between running a business or pursuing a career and economic theory as it exists today. But it can be a financially fatal error to shrug off economics as pointless if you want to make money in the financial markets. It is the designs of theoretical economists and the alleged solutions to economic problems instituted by bureaucrats and members of Congress that largely determine the long-term course of business activity and the direction of price movements.

If you already watch the markets. You have seen equities debt, and futures prices respond dramatically to news of the level of the new budget deficit to the Federal Reserve Board's policy regarding the availability of money and credit to reports on the Treasury Department's policy relating to the value of the dollar abroad or to rumors of new trade legislation. The markets concede that the government holds the club that can break the back of American business. A huge part of successful speculation and investment now rests on anticipating the nature and effects of government fiscal policy, monetary policy, and interventionist legislation on specific markets and on the general business cycle.

Our economy operates according to market principles, but the government sets the stage, and it's a secret, rotating stage subject to change at any moment. But if you understand the errors in the economic theory that motivate the stage managers, you can anticipate the new set and position yourself to act profitably. Therefore, understanding economics has everything to do with successful speculation and investment; it provides the foundation for any good system of market forecasting. Let me put that last statement in perspective.

I went to Indiana University and Harvard Business School to study business but found it almost entirely worthless except in a reverse sense; that is, I gained knowledge of what is wrong with conventional economic thinking rather than what is right.

My formal schooling gave me an understanding of the predominantly Keynesian ideas that our government uses in making policy decisions. Studying on my own, however, I discovered that the conventional wisdom taught in most universities was contradicted by thinkers such as Adam Smith, Ludwig von Mises, Frederick Hayek, Henry Hazlitt, Ayn Rand, and others. I learned that Keynes was little more than a sophisticated mercantilist and a bubble builder.

I don't think you need formal schooling to obtain the economic knowledge needed to succeed in the financial markets. In fact, I encouraged a brilliant young man who trades for me not to go to college by offering him a job and telling him that he could learn what he needs to know about the markets much better and faster on his own than he could in most university systems. Through observation and experience, he is learning how the world works and is rapidly becoming an exceptional trader.

On the other hand, I know of a securities analyst, an economics major with five years' experience at a major firm, who, when asked if he thought the U.S. government debt would ever be paid off, replied, "No, it will probably continue to grow." When then asked how long the debt could continue to grow without lenders losing confidence in the government's ability to repay, he replied, "I don't know, but eventually they'll just have to write it off. After all, it's just paper!" Just paper!!?? He'll watch in horror in the next bear market when bonds and stocks keep making lower lows. Unfortunately, judging from the countless number of people I have talked to with similar views, this kind of thinking is the rule rather than the exception, and it is traceable to a poor or misguided understanding of basic economic principles.

You can't reverse cause and effect. The so-called economic "gurus" in Washington can't create prosperity with the stroke of a pen on a new bill in Congress. Economics isn't a magical realm nor the province of geniuses or specialists with some unique insight akin to religious revelation. Many policy makers are little more than political cowards who are afraid to tell special interest groups that they can't have something for nothing. Instead, they develop elaborate schemes to try to cheat reality by overspending, while evading or ignoring the inevitable results of their programs-inflation or recession. And they do it in the name of economic principles.

In his book "new economics," John Maynard Keynes formalized and gave quasi-scientific status to economic fallacies that are as old as civilized man. He provided a rationalization for government intervention into free markets for government control of the supply of money and credit, and for policies of irresponsible deficit spending and inflationary expansionism. With very few exceptions the intellectual community has taken his fallacies as axiomatic principles and expanded them into a hopelessly complex system of terms, symbols, and mathematical equations. It is no wonder that most people are either bored or intimidated by the study of economics.

If you are bored or intimidated by economics, it is partly because politicians and members of academia have for years been declaring that our society and the inter-workings of the markets have become too complicated for the average man to cope with on his own. The "complex economic issues" of our modern world, they contend, must be carefully weighed against one another, and a balance must be struck between the "ideal" and the "practical."

They foster the view that only government, supported by countless task forces, high-paid consultants, and many subcommittees and bureaucratic agencies can find the right set of "compromises" to manage the mixed bag of interests in our nation. They allege that the government should control the economy by inflating the supply of money and credit to encourage production, while simultaneously taxing the "excess profits" of the most productive industries; by deficit spending to provide the "underprivileged" with "equal opportunity. "All while forcing the businesses that might have been able to employ them to provide minimum wages, matching social security contributions, and unemployment insurance; by imposing trade barriers to encourage domestic industry, while simultaneously providing "developing" third world countries with low cost loans or outright grants so that they will be our "friends". Subsidizing the price of wheat, sugar, soybeans, milk and other agricultural products to "maintain the independence and competitiveness of the American farmer," while giving away the surpluses or selling them at a loss to foreign nations; and the list goes on and on.

My genuine reaction to this view is not fit for print, so I'll temper it by saying: "Don't let them fool you!" If you balance your checkbook each month and understand that you can't operate with a negative balance indefinitely, you already know more about economics than most government policy makers. They and their many different programs and laws, which cost American producers a huge percentage of their income each year, are just shapeless, colorless pieces in a puzzle with no meaningful solution. But with the right knowledge, you can make those pieces fit into your puzzle; you can turn government irrationality into dollars in the bank.

As a trader, speculator, or investor you make money by buying and selling market instruments in anticipation of price changes or value appreciation and depreciation. To do this well, you have to acquire a basic understanding of why people exchange things, what a market is, who participates in it, how prices are determined, why price changes occur, what will bring them about when they will happen, and so on. Also, because government intervention into the markets causes more price volatility than any single factor, you have to understand how public policy affects market conditions. Like a journalist seeking the truth in writing a story, you have to ask and answer the questions: Who? What? When? Where? Why? And How? Answering these questions on a general, fundamental level is the province of economics. Answering them in particular for a specific market is the area of market forecasting. Economics provides the basic ideas needed for accurate market forecasting.

Armed with the right basic economic principles, you can develop a logical method of market forecasting, rip through the masses of data, and discard the trash that will burden you when making decisions. You can start with a single correct idea, observe market data, and derive conclusions that are both sensible and accurate. You can listen to the opinions of the analysts and "experts" and test their findings according to basic premises that are unchanging in their validity, knowing that where there are contradictions, there are mistakes. In short, you can compete effectively with people who have much more particularized knowledge than you do.

It's not how many facts you know but the truth and quality of what you know that counts. I know a man who I watched answer every single question on Jeopardy correctly-and yet he blew out as a trader. He spent countless hours developing ingenious but faulty strategies to predict market behavior. I admire the man's raw intellectual capability, but he has a problem when it comes to trading-he has never identified the basic principles which govern market behavior.

The purpose of this chapter is to determine and define the basic principles and terms of economics so that later, I can show you how to apply them to anticipate changes in the business cycle and make money with your knowledge. Like the sides of the puzzle box, these principles act as the guidelines for piecing together the puzzle of market forecasting.

ECONOMICS

I place economy among the first and most important virtues and public debt among the greatest of dangers; we must make our choice between economy and liberty; or profusion and servitude. If we can prevent the government from wasting the labors of the people under the pretense of caring for them, they will be happy.

-Thomas Jefferson

In this statement, Jefferson used the term "economy" in two slightly different senses. When he said the economy was "among the first and most important virtues," he meant careful and thrifty management of public revenue. When he said we have to choose between economy and liberty, he was addressing the question of where the focus of government should be whether the government should expand its purse and provide public services or focus on protecting life, liberty, and property.

Jefferson understood better than any political leader in world history that government "profusion" can only be paid by "the labors of the people." He knew that a growing government budget and an extension of the services government offers "under the pretense of caring for [the people]" can only come at the expense of private property and individual liberty.

Unfortunately, over the last two centuries the people of this nation, through the selection of their political leaders, have chosen profusion over liberty to the extent that many of us now labor about one day out of every three to pay for government extravagance. And even that is not enough. With deficits consistently higher than $100 billion a year, future generations will inherit a financial burden that, if not arrested soon, will be impossible to bear. Jefferson has probably worn holes in his funeral clothes turning over in his grave.

We've reached this state because bad ideas, not just economic ideas but philosophical ideas, have been adopted and put into practice. Americans have been tricked into thinking that there is no absolute right and wrong-only a balance of relative elements, that life is enormously complex and nothing is simple, and that therefore it is best to leave economic policy in the hands of the "experts."

I am not writing a philosophical treatise, but nothing is more complete than life or death, and life means economic survival. I won't tell you that everything is simple, but I will tell you that most things are not as complicated as they seem. I can't describe every mistaken economic notion and then refute it, but I can supply you with the basic definitions and principles that I know are right and appeal to logic and the size of my bank account, not the conventional wisdom, for confirmation. So let me start from scratch by answering the question, "What is economics?"

Economics is the study of a branch of human action. According to economist Ludwig von Mises, "It is the science of the means to be applied for the attainment of ends chosen; . . . . [It] is not about things and tangible material objects; it is about men, their meanings, and actions. "In other words, it is the study of the instruments, methods, and activities available to human beings for attaining their goals. This definition serves as the first principle of economic analysis and market forecasting; understanding it is a prerequisite for integrating all other principles into a unified, coherent system and profiting from your knowledge.

Most economics texts would define economics more like this: the study of the "production, distribution, and use of income, wealth, and commodities. "While it is true that economics is concerned with these things, this is not an accurate definition. It implies, for example, that income and commodities already exist and that they stand apart from wealth. It assumes a level of development such that distribution is a major concern. In short, it assumes that people exist at a high degree of sophistication in society, when in fact that very sophistication is the result of fundamental economic principles that apply first to the individual, even if he is alone on an island.

Consider, for example, Daniel Defoe's character Robinson Crusoe. His actions demonstrate concretely the fundamentals of individual economic behavior that lead to the formation of a market economy. Stranded on an island visited only by cannibalistic savages, Crusoe first devised a method of acquiring more food than he immediately needed and stored it so that he could redirect his efforts toward achieving other necessities. He used the time he saved to build shelter, provide for his defense against the natives, and manufacture clothing. Then through industry, ingenuity, and management of time, he simplified the process of acquiring essentials and went on to produce other luxuries as time allowed.

The keys to the process of increasing his standard of living were the evaluation, production, saving, investment, and innovation. He evaluated the ends and means available to him and chose the alternatives that best addressed his needs. The value of each thing that he sought was set by his judgment according to his perception of what was most needed, the means available to obtain it, and what it would cost him to get it relative to the alternatives. He produced the essentials necessary for survival and saved enough of them so that he could invest his energy into developing other products that he needed or desired. The price he paid at each step was the time and energy he spent according to his evaluation of his needs. What he gained on balance in the exchange was his profit. If he made mistakes, and his efforts were futile, he suffered a loss. His actions were a matter of trade, the exchange of a less desirable state for a more desirable one. At every step, he managed his time; he made choices based on the consequences of his options in the short, intermediate, and long term. As he became more and more sophisticated through technological innovation, the cost of essentials diminished and he could afford to spend more of his time in the pursuit of "luxuries."

The concepts I've emphasized in explaining Crusoe's actions are associated with measures and results in a market economy. In fact, a market economy is simply the product of the same concepts applied in a social context. Evaluation, production, saving, investment, and innovation are requirements for man's survival and growth according to his nature as an individual, rational human being.

Properly considered, economics is the study of the means available to sustain life as a person, and because people are social creatures, a primary emphasis must be on surviving through association with others. But the fundamental focus must be on the requirements of one individual standing alone, as a society is simply a collection of individuals.

What is a Market?

The fundamental means of survival available to a group are the same as they are for one person. The only significant differences arise from the degree of complexity with which the actions of production and exchange are performed. The individual acting alone can exchange one state of affairs for another, but only through the expense of his energy.

Within a free society, he can exchange the product of his effort for the goods and services of others, gaining enormous benefits through the division of labor, specialization, and the innovation of others. Thus, a market economy makes survival easier, but through more sophisticated means than any one person can achieve alone. Economic activity is more complex concerning the resources and choices available; but in terms of survival and growth, it is much simpler. Crusoe couldn't have survived by acting as the janitor on his island, but there are many people who make a decent living washing the windows of skyscrapers in New York City.

Given knowledge as elementary as Crusoe's, and if protected from coercion by others, people attempt to trade their property by voluntary consent to their advantage. They evaluate the products and services offered for trade, and based on their ability to strike a bargain, choose those that are deemed most needed or desirable. On each side of the trade, one person exchanges something judged to be of lesser value for something judged to be of greater value. The trade is a matter of individual judgment, of each, estimate of the value of holding one item versus another. The process of evaluation is necessarily subjective: that is, it depends on each person's specific preferences, judgment, values, and goals.

The fact that value is subjective-that people appreciate things differently-both drives people to trade and makes it possible for both sides to profit.' The farmer who has excess corn but not enough meat values his surplus corn less than the rancher who needs corn to fatten his cattle-the opportunity for a trade exists. As more and more people associate and get involved in the process of exchanging their surpluses, trading becomes more complicated. The interaction of numerous individuals, the social device of production and trade through free association, is called a market.

A market is the means people use to engage in the voluntary exchange of property according to the law of supply and demand. This definition applies equally to a local flea market and the New York Stock Exchange. The system of exchange may be simple or complex, but the defining characteristic of a market as such is that it is composed of a group of individuals engaged in trade-engaged in the process of trying to exchange property in their self-interest.

THE ROLE OF MONEY

Money is necessary only after members of the marketplace have achieved a high level of productivity and long-term control over their lives. In its essential form, money is simply a commodity which is so desirable that it is acceptable to virtually anyone in an intermediate exchange. It is no less a commodity than pickled herring, but it has a longer shelf life (durability), has a universally recognized value, is divisible, and is portable. Money so simplifies the process of exchange that direct barter becomes unnecessary. It makes economic calculation possible; it provides a means for people to translate the inherently subjective hierarchy of their economic values into numeric terms. And it provides a means of quantifying and saving the surplus of products over consumption. By accepting dollars or gold, an individual relies on its buying power in the future, whether that be minutes, days, or years. Thus, money is a product which serves as a medium of exchange and a store of value, but which is no more and no less subject to the laws of supply and demand than any other product or service.

Another form of money arose from a sophistication in the extension of credit. Credit is a market innovation created to utilize the otherwise idle savings of individuals. In the early history of credit, when gold and silver were the accepted money, the metal itself was loaned (usually secured by specified collateral) in return for a promise to pay the original amount borrowed plus interest. Then an innovation was created-the money certificate or bank note.

Lenders discovered that a certificate promising to redeem to the bearer a specified amount of gold or silver was a suitable and convenient medium of exchange. Once these certificates were recognized as acceptable due to the soundness and reputation of the financial institution which issued them, it didn't take a genius to realize that more certificates could be issued than actual deposits of hard currency, and fiduciary media were created.

As long as the issuer carefully scrutinized the prospects of repayment and maintained a reputation of soundness with depositors, it could create money substitutes (bank notes and money certificates) by extending credit beyond the limits of its hard currency deposits. In this way, and for the first time, the rate of growth of wealth could be accelerated beyond that possible by loaning hard currency-all based on the lender's judgment of the borrower's ability to produce and trade in the future.

When the government stayed out of it, the growth of fiduciary media was regulated primarily by market factors.' That is, the bank was ultimately liable to redeem all outstanding notes in gold or silver, so the quantity of precious metal deposits provided an objective standard and a check on the limit of credit expansion. Like any other business, some banks prospered, and other banks failed; and some depositors earned interest on their savings, and other investors lost everything. But overall, the innovation of extending credit beyond actual savings dramatically accelerated the growth of wealth.

Today, fiat money-paper declared to be legal tender by the government is the accepted medium of exchange. Fiat money is similar to fiduciary media in the sense that the currency itself has no use except as a medium of exchange, but it is different in that there is no objective value backing it. In a fiat money system the government, not market factors, determines the supply of money and credit. The objective limits are gone, replaced by the subjective limits imposed by government bureaucrats.

The banking system holds reserves not as precious metals, but as demands for government notes9 secured by the power to tax and print money. 1° by stipulating fractional reserve requirements for lending, buying, and selling government money market instruments, and manipulating interest rates, government central banks set the limits of credit availability. These limits largely determine the level of borrowing by businesses and consumers, which in turn establishes the rate of growth or decline of the money supply.

Even though the supply of money and credit are government controlled, market principles still govern the purchasing power of money and the cost of credit. Money and credit are still subject to the law of supply and demand, but the supply side of the equation is manipulated. And savings are still the basis for sound business expansion through the prudent extension of credit.

Credit, if properly managed, accelerates the growth of wealth because it provides the most efficient use of savings and the potential productive capacity of individuals and institutions. Money saved is a claim on unconsumed goods. Savers choose to forgo immediate consumption in favor of future consumption or investment. Through the advent of credit, they can make a deal, either directly or through the institution holding their money, to let others borrow their savings for consumption or investment in return for a promise of greater purchasing power in the future. Borrowers use the loan to purchase unconsumed goods either for consumption or investment, but either way, they are obligated to create enough new wealth to pay back the loan plus interest. The lending institution creates new money when it makes the loan, but if the money is not repaid out of newly created wealth, then actual savings are consumed.

What Is Wealth?

Wealth is simply an accumulation of products and services which are both available and wanted for consumption. The only way to create wealth is to produce more than is consumed, which is made possible through technology. Technology is an applied science, and science means knowledge. People increase their productivity by acquiring new knowledge and applying it. In many ways, our lives are so abundant that this fact is easy to forget. We take for granted the efficiencies introduced in the market through innovations such as specialization, the division of labor, and mechanization. These were all discoveries, ideas in the creative minds of individual people that were transformed into reality. In a market economy, everyone gains from the creator's innovation. The efficiencies gained through technological innovation cascade through the market so that each person can produce more in less time. As each individual produces more, he or she can consume more, according to the law of supply and demand.

No matter how sophisticated the products and services become, no matter how many people get involved in the process, the principles that Crusoe employed on his island remain immutable. To live, one must evaluate what is required or desired to enhance life, and produce in order to acquire it. The price one pays is what one must give up in order to obtain the desired item. To accumulate wealth, one must save so that time and intermediate products can be invested in acquiring other goods. To diversify one's labor requires innovation, which increases the time efficiency of one's industry.

ECONOMICS AND HUMAN NATURE

Business is like a man rowing a boat upstream. He has no choice; he must go ahead, or he will go back.

-Lewis E. Pierson

A free market economy is a human invention based on a view of humanity as consisting of independent, rational beings capable of providing for their survival. It is an invention, but one which arises spontaneously, as a natural result of individuals acting reasonably and uncoerced in a social setting. Governments don't create markets; they take them away through effective intervention. If government leaves its citizens alone, markets arise automatically, almost as if they have a life of their own.

As evidence, I offer the fact that even in societies where production and trade are tightly controlled by autocratic or collectivist regimes, "black" markets are rampant and are most often silently sanctioned and even patronized by the authorities. For example, a recent television program about Poland explained how the local government in a small city took a few acres of land and divided it into small plots (smaller than the back yard which many American suburbanites take for granted) and distributed them to families so they could grow vegetables for their consumption. Almost immediately, the rights to use the plots were trading on the silently sanctioned black market for amounts far exceeding the average yearly earnings of a Polish family. The reason? Fresh fruit and vegetables were (and I presume still are) practically nonexistent in the state-run markets but sold on the black market for premium prices. A family that acquired a few plots instead of one and produced small crops for sale in the private market could more than double their yearly income.

While such "gray markets" spring up any time trading in a highly desired item is restricted by any government, the idea of markets as such is condemned in collectivist regimes. For example, in Russia, an entirely different set of principles is derived from the study of "the means applied to the attainment of ends chosen." Human beings are viewed not as independent beings existing for their own sake, but as a disposable natural resource designed to serve the greater whole-the state or the collective. By this view, to act as Crusoe did to improve his standard of living is self-fulfilling and therefore opposed to the fundamental communist tenet "from each according to his ability, to each according to his need." In any issue, the "common good" is the standard of value; and the "collective wisdom," as interpreted by self-appointed guardians, is the final judge of truth and falsehood."

For them, the concepts of value, price, investment, and innovation have entirely different meaning and focus. Bureaucrats attempt to set value by government dictate, and price by decree. State planners invest resources without regard for profit. They try to make people work without personal incentive or potential for substantial self-improvement. And the result is a society of people so tired of living at a subsistence level that its political leaders are, at this writing, in the process of removing many market constraints for fear of total economic collapse and political rebellion.

I bring up what may seem to be political issues for a fundamental reason. You can't separate economic thinking from a view of the nature of human beings. The dominant philosophic view of humanity in any culture will determine the nature of its political structure and therefore the nature of its economic activity. The closer that profound view comes to being correct, the more successful economic policy will be. The extent that people are seen as rational beings, not infallible but capable of providing for their own survival with actions based on the independent exercise of their minds, is the extent to which the society will be free and unfettered by government intervention. And the degree to which a society is free is the extent to which it will be successful in terms of a general and increasing rise in the standard of living of its people. Unfortunately, there are strong collectivist elements in every nation in the world, including the United States. To some extent, people are universally regarded as being responsible not just for their own lives, but also for the welfare of others.

The purpose of government, according to collectivist ideology, is to provide for the common good through dynamic redistribution of wealth from those who produce to those who can't (or won't), or to those who don't produce as much. Consequently, markets in the United States and worldwide are, in varying degrees, regulated and controlled.

In particular, the supply of money and credit is entirely in politicians' hands, and therefore the markets are largely at the mercy of bureaucratic whim. But just as a good detective can apprehend a criminal by taking on his mindset, so it is possible to grasp the course of government policy by taking on the mindset of key figures in power. The extent to which they are collectivist is the degree to which they will intervene in the markets and create imbalances of varying forms. By examining the effects of their interventionist policies on production, savings, investment, and innovation and by analyzing the impact on supply and demand in the various markets, you can predict the direction of price movements.

To anticipate future economic policy, you must understand the policy weapons available, as well as the character and intent of the men in crucial positions of power. In the United States, the most fundamental policy weapons are taxes, the level and method of funding deficit spending, the Federal Reserve Board's control of money and credit, and specific laws restricting production and trade. The leading personalities to observe are the President, the Fed Chairman, the Secretary of the Treasury, and key Congressional leaders. By understanding first what these men can do, and then anticipating what they might do based on their view of the nature of human beings, you can position yourself to profit from future government action.

Analyzing effects is much simpler than anticipating new policy.

Government interference in the economy has consequences directed by distinctly market principles. One simple principle is: Price controls cause shortages, and price supports cause surpluses. For example, when Ronald Reagan was elected in 1980, the domestic oil production industry was enjoying a government-stimulated boom brought about by tariffs on imported oil, an artificial shortage induced by the OPEC cartel, and an elaborate system of price controls and tax benefits created by the Carter Administration which put a price limit on "old oil" but let the price of newly produced oil float. There was a drilling frenzy everyone was speculating on oil wells. ~

After his election, Reagan announced a plan to deregulate the oil industry. A good friend of mine and fantastic broker told me this story over a few drinks. Shortly after that, I got a call from a stock broker friend of mine who urged me to buy Tom Brown, an over-the-counter oil stock that had enjoyed a mercurial rise from $2 a share to about $68 a share. I told him, "Jimmy, it's over for the oil industry; I might want to short that stock." He pleaded with me not to short it because Tom Brown was a friend of his, so I didn't, but I did short many other oil stocks.

I told Jimmy that the oil cartel in the Mideast would soon collapse from competitive pressure and that Reagan's proposed deregulation would kill the domestic oil industry as free competition drove prices down. He slowed down his purchasing but held on to his positions hoping to close them out in 1981 for tax reasons. By January 1981, however, his oil portfolio was down about 25%. The S&P 500 index, which was heavily weighted by the oil stocks, topped in November 1980. Tom Brown eventually dropped back to about $2. I profited handsomely by acting on straightforward principles.

Now let me project into the future a little bit using the same principles. The recent increase in the legal minimum wage will decrease the profitability of fast food stores and other retail outlets, forcing some out of business and others to lay off workers. Automation devices will enjoy increased use as they become relatively more valuable due to the increased cost of labor. Unemployment among the unskilled labor force and youth will increase, and the demand for government assistance programs will increase. "In the name of caring for the people," the government will once again contribute to the impoverishment of the nation. Government intervention doesn't circumvent the laws of supply and demand; it simply maldistributed factors on both sides of the equation.

To reiterate, economics is important because it describes the instruments, methods, and activities human beings employ to achieve ends or goals. The focus of economics must be first on the individual acting alone, and then on the individual acting in a social setting. The principles that apply to one person apply equally to any group and society as a whole. For economic principles to be correct, they must be based on a view of humans as independent, thinking beings in pursuit of their own fulfillment. Any other view will lead to contradictions-mistaken judgments that fail when action is taken based on them. Like Robinson Crusoe, everyone must understand the concepts of evaluation, production, savings, investment, and innovation in order to survive and flourish as human beings. For the trader, speculator, and investor, a more detailed knowledge of these principles is an indispensable tool for market forecasting, particularly for evaluating the effects of government intervention on price movements.

PRODUCTION BEFORE AFFLUENCE

Suppose you went to work for someone, and every day you just sat and drank coffee, checked social media, and doodled on company stationery. How long do you think you would last? Not long, for sure. Your employer would justifiably fire you for not contributing anything of value to the business-for not producing anything.

It is an inescapable fact that human beings have to produce in order to survive and prosper. Production is the act of bringing something new into existence, by recombination and rearrangement of natural and man-made elements, which is designed for a particular purpose. By the phrase "bringing something new into existence" I don't mean to imply that something can come from nothing. What was a fish, the fisherman turns to food; by his actions and innovation, he brings food into being. What was steel, copper, aluminum, plastic, textiles, and so on, the auto maker turns into a car. The film producer combines the director, actors, writers, and crew to make a movie for entertainment, advertisement, or education. The doctor attempts to produce the health of his patient. The stock trader brings into being an evaluation and exchange. I'm sure you get my point.

The act of production can be simple or complex-from gathering food to the manufacture of plastics from refined oil derivatives. The products can range from biological necessities to abstract ideas-from food to poetry-but in each case, something new is created that is intended to serve a predefined goal or end. Some all too influential pressure groups condemn production beyond a certain point. They say that through "overproduction" humanity is progressing farther and farther away from its "natural state" and speak of the "simplicity and beauty" of the few remaining food-gathering tribes in remote regions of the world. For example, the organization manual of Friends of the Earth declares, "The only excellent technology is no technology at all," further stating that economic development is "taxation without representation imposed by an elitist species upon the rest of the natural world. Others refer wistfully to the fabled "Garden of Eden" as man's ideal state and hold that productive work is humanity's punishment for seeking knowledge of good and evil.

Can you imagine living your life dependent on fickle mother nature, spending each day hunting and gathering food in never ending repetition? Can you imagine living in a "paradise" where no thought and no action were required, in which "to produce" was inconsequential and irrelevant? What would be your source of pleasure and happiness if all your provisions for survival and all decisions were predetermined-if alternatives were neither necessary nor possible? Whatever this sort of "paradise" would be, it could hardly be called a "human' existence, and I would have no desire to take part in it. I have to wonder why some people regard a beaver dam as "natural," but not the New York skyline-both ate the result of animals acting according to their nature.

The basis of production is, in Ayn Rand's words, " the application of reason to the problem of survival." People survive through the use of their minds; by identifying their requirements and desires, ordering them according to the evaluation of their relative importance, discovering the means to achieve them and taking productive action. Unlike other animals, people create their environment by remolding nature following its laws. They can lift themselves out of nature's harshness, make scarce necessities abundant, prolong human life, and open whole new frontiers of challenge and opportunity. But they can do this only as long as they are free to produce.

I have carefully defined production to include all purposeful action that results in the attainment of a goal or value in an attempt to dispel a mistaken notion, widespread in economic thinking, that only action which results in the creation of material goods is "productive." Many economists divide the industry into the productive sector and the service sector as if those who provide services aren't productive. Some lament the growth of automation and mechanization was saying that it is forcing labor to move into the service sector and that therefore the pool of skilled and educated labor will continue to decline. Services, they declare, act only to redistribute wealth rather than generate it. This is a very short-sighted and mistaken view that arises from a mistaken concept of economic value and wealth.

Economic value is anything that fulfills a need, is recognized as such, and is attainable-which includes both commodities and services. I use "need" here in the widest sense to mean that which is required, desired, or wanted; and I assume that only one person can determine the need-the individual. If enough individuals want and are willing to pay for the same economic value, then it has market value.

It is a business's goal to recognize or create market value and profit by satisfying consumers' desires. In pursuing this goal, businessmen use mechanization, automation, and other innovations to make more products and services available to more people at a lower price. The laborers who are temporarily displaced by technological improvements may move into the service industry, but they may also be absorbed by the manufacturers of the sophisticated capital goods which make mechanization and automation possible. No matter which, both are a new source of wealth. The savings gained in mechanization are invested in new products and services, and the net wealth of the nation is increased. You might call it nature's way of upgrading and improving humanity. New, more economical methods of production replace old ways, forcing people at all levels of society to upgrade their knowledge and skills in order to compete in the markets.

While there are strong factions, especially in organized labor, that would prefer stagnation to growth, those who embrace change and continually expand their knowledge are likely to grow, not only financially, but also personally. Constantly thinking, learning, and producing are fundamental requirements for gaining a sense of self-esteem and self-worth. If this fact were more widely understood and applied, it would contribute to a healthier, happier, and more productive culture.

The idea that the service industry is unproductive is unfounded. Beyond attaining the subsistence commodities of food, shelter, and clothing, there is an unlimited number of options available for individuals to dispose of the products of their efforts; to use their wealth. If they choose to spend money in an expensive restaurant, they are consuming their wealth, but in so doing helping to pay the construction workers who built the structure, the landlord who owns it, the furniture manufacturer who built the tables and chairs, the wages of the waiter who serves them, and so forth. Their consumption supports, in part, the ability of countless others to produce.

Economists often divide the nation into "producers" and "consumers" as if they were a different species, perhaps even at odds with one another. While this division has some value for analytical purposes, actually every producer is a consumer, and every consumer is a producer. The man who works in an automobile assembly plant contributes to the creation of the finished product. Even though his role is an intermediary in the process, he is nonetheless productive. The same goes for a waitress in a restaurant- she creates a portion of the atmosphere and service that is paid for. These people are wage earners, producers who trade their product for wages, and then, in turn, trade their salaries for the goods and services of others. For each individual, the simultaneous role of producer and consumer-the chain of action consisting of produce and trade, produce and trade is the only way people can legitimately achieve their ends in a free market economy.

To produce is to create potential wealth. Wealth is an accumulation of unconsumed goods, whether products or services-anything that is considered to be of value by individuals in the marketplace. In this sense, a waiter's as yet unused services are wealth. The fact that today we measure wealth in monetary terms does not change its essential nature. An accumulation of money is simply an accumulation of claims on market goods and services, but one which varies in value over time.

The measure of success in the marketplace is the ability to accumulate wealth by either creating or anticipating the demand for one's products or services at a price that will sustain not only survival but economic growth. Production is the first step in this process; saving is the next.

SAVINGS, INVESTMENT, CREDIT, AND WEALTH

While production is the prerequisite to survival, savings is the prerequisite for economic growth. Accumulating wealth is the first step is to produce more than is required for immediate consumption. Then, two alternatives are possible: the surplus can is stored for use at a later date, which is called plain saving; or the stored product can be used either to enhance future productivity or for sustenance, while working toward ends that take longer to achieve, which is called capital saving or capital accumulation.

With everyday saving, products are set aside but sooner or later will be consumed leaving nothing in their place. With capital saving, goods are accumulated which are designed for either improving the production process or creating new products altogether. It is capital savings which lead to the improvement of man's material condition and frees him to enhance life further, not only by learning and producing more but also by enjoying leisure and recreational activities. Capital saving is an investment in the future, and in this way, savings is an investment.

Saving is an act of choice based on a discounting of the value of consuming future products against the value of consuming existing products. The ratio of the value assigned to existing products and the value allocated to future products is called original interests-it is a measure of the interest in consuming now versus consuming later. The higher original interest is, the lower will be the rate of capital savings, and conversely, the lower it is, the higher will be the rate of capital accumulation and therefore the rate of growth of wealth.

Originary interest shows itself in the financial markets through the rate of growth or decline of capital goods, 16 which is directly tied to the level of individual savings and the supply of and demand for credit. Capital accumulation is not directly tied to the interest rate. The market interest rate is the cost of credit of which original interest is only one component. But original interest is the underlying driving force which determines whether people will consume now or later. It varies from person to person and is dependent on a broad range of conditions. The reason for this distinction will become apparent when I discuss the effects of monetary policy on the business cycle in the next chapter. Ultimately, the decision to save is based on the ability and desire to forgo consumption now in exchange for higher returns in the future; it is the choice not to consume today at the expense of growth tomorrow.

The engine of growth is new technology, which arises from creative innovation and the investment of knowledge, time, energy, and resources gained through savings. Technology is applied knowledge, and innovation is an act of creation. Therefore, technological innovation is the act of creating new ways to use knowledge. The first fisherman who thought of catching fish with a net was an innovator, and the net was his new technology. In effect, the net was a form of savings-a capital good used to simplify the process of production.

The first net fisherman had to save in order to acquire the knowledge, time, energy, and materials to construct the net. Once he created the net and learned how to use it, he saved enormous amounts of productive energy by making each of his working hours more fruitful. He could not only provide fish for himself and his family but could trade his surplus for the products of others. Fish became less scarce because they required less labor to attain, and therefore his neighbors could afford to specialize in producing other necessities to trade with him for his fish. This example, on a primitive scale, shows how the efficiencies gained from one man's saving, innovation, investment, and capital accumulation filter through the community and make everyone more productive.

At each step in the progress of civilization, we inherit the knowledge of other people and improve on it. This too is a form of savings that leads to growth. We inherit the canoe and make a sailboat. The sailboat becomes a steamship. The steamship becomes a diesel-powered supertanker. And so on. Underpinning the whole process is the savings and preparatory work arising from earlier generations and ultimately from the creativity of individuals. If our fishing ancestors had utterly consumed their nets and canoes without bothering to invest the time to replace them; if our ancestors hadn't passed down the knowledge of how to grow wheat and make flour; if human beings, like other animals, were pure consumers, civilization as we know it would not exist. It is savings, of products and of knowledge, which makes investment and growth possible.

It is easy to see at a primitive level of social development how saving makes investment possible. It is not so easy to see the process at work in a complex market economy. For example, when a manufacturing company borrows money to invest in capital goods such as new and more efficient machinery, it is difficult to see where savings come into play. It is so difficult in fact that economists like John Maynard Keynes convinced other influential economists and government policy makers that production and savings are not the prerequisites for growth.

In Keynesian terms, aggregate demand, as measured in dollars of disposable income, is the driving force behind the production. Put a few extra dollars into everyone's hand, he said, and they'll spend it, thereby increasing demand and inducing industry to produce more. Savings, on the contrary, promotes "underconsumption," takes away from aggregate demand, diminishes the GNP, and stifles growth. According to this view, the government can guarantee prosperity by pumping money into the economy through deficit spending and easy credit policies and by encouraging spending rather than saving. The problem for Keynesian thinkers is simply one of careful management of public expenditure and the money supply.

I mentioned earlier that money serves as a medium of exchange and a store of value, and that when someone saves money, he or she is withholding claims against unconsumed goods and services. On the surface of it, based on these two observations, it may seem that saving is unproductive, that in fact savings and investment are not directly tied. You might argue that by not buying anything, the saver reduces demand for the products available on the market, diminishes the profits of industry, and therefore contributes to a decline in business activity. Nothing could be further from the truth.

Consider the two basic types of savers: the miser who stuffs money into the mattress, and the typical saver who puts money into a bank or some other instrument such as bonds, gold, or stocks. There aren't many Scrooges in the world who hoard money in mattresses for no other reason than for the love of holding it. But to the extent that this happens, the result is a reduction in the supply of money in circulation relative to other commodities, producing a downward pressure on prices and an increase in the purchasing power of money. Remember that money is a commodity no more and no less subject to the laws of supply and demand than any other commodity. If supply is diminished, its value relative to other products will go up. Wealth cannot be equated with a quantity of money without regard to the purchasing power of money.

In the last few decades of the nineteenth century, industrial expansion and the standard of living in the United States grew at the fastest rate in the history of the world, before or since. But an economist measuring wealth in terms of dollars wouldn't necessarily recognize this. Over a 20-year period, during the height of the expansionary period, the gold and silver-based money supply remained relatively stable, and the general level of prices fell about 50%. In fact, throughout the eighteenth and nineteenth centuries, except during war time when the government financed expenditures through the issue of paper money, declining prices were the rule, not the exception.

Today, because we are so completely indoctrinated to our government's inflationary monetary policy, this seems almost bizarre. But if you think of money as a commodity, then it makes sense. Just as business people today attempt to account for continually rising prices in their pricing and return calculations, so business people used to anticipate the effects of falling prices. Businesses increased profits during periods of declining dollar revenues because the value of the dollar was steadily increasing.

The difference is that market factors, not the government, were the principal determinant of the supply of money and credit.

Many modern economists equate falling prices with economic decline. The reason is that since the late 1920s the only time the general level of prices has dropped is during periods of depression or recession. A careful examination of these periods will show government intervention at its worst. For example, in the 1930s, the Federal Reserve Board reduced the money supply by one-third while Congress simultaneously passed legislation to maintain prices at 1920s levels. Farmers were paid to burn potatoes and plow under cotton crops to create high prices. Merchants were rewarded with a "Blue Eagle" insignia in their windows if they adhered to artificially high government price guidelines, and Roosevelt in his "fireside chats" encouraged consumers to shop only at Blue Eagle stores and to snitch on merchants who violated the guidelines. Labor legislation empowered and encouraged unions to increase their wage demands and stopped industries from instituting wage reductions. The result was that real wages rose during a period of declining output and widespread unemployment. For some reason, it never dawned on government officials that a decrease in the money supply would necessarily result in lower prices! The result, of course, was the most prolonged recession in U.S. economic history.

Our government's spending and monetary policy alternates between inflationary booms driven by easy credit policies, followed by busts resulting from the tightening of money and credit to control inflation. It is our government's policies of deficit spending and oversight of the money supply through the Federal Reserve system that makes it virtually impossible for modern Americans to imagine prosperity during a period of price declines. But wouldn't it be incredible to be able to put money in the bank and have its purchasing power increase without worrying about price inflation? Can you imagine how fast the prices of high-tech items would drop when you combined the effects of technological improvements, competition, and deflating prices because of the increasing purchasing power of the dollar? The major point is that business declines are not caused by, and do not necessarily have anything to do with, falling prices.

The miser, at worst, by removing money from circulation can have only a limited effect on prices and the markets. Assuming that the money supply is static, prices will eventually adjust to a higher level as the result of his actions. If the money supply is continually increasing relative to other goods and services, as is presently true, then his money will lose purchasing power. If a miser stuffed a million dollars into his mattress in 1940, it would today be worth only $120,000 in terms of relative purchasing power. So the miser only hurts himself with his hoarding.

There are many alleged justifications for government regulation of money and credit, but among the most influential is Keynes' argument that saving is unproductive-that business declines are caused by "underconsumption," which means hoarding. For years, saving has been equated with hoarding, but I have just shown that the most foolish of misers do no damage except to himself by stuffing money into his mattress.

The average saver is not a miser, but rather puts money into the bank or into other institutions and instruments which make savings available for use in the credit market. This kind of saver entrusts another person or organization to keep his money in return for the benefits to be derived from their management of his savings. It is this kind of savings that provides the fuel for an expanding economy. Also, the higher the level of savings, the lower the cost of credit-it's a simple matter of supply and demand.

The principle is no different than Crusoe saving food so he would have time to build a shelter. It just happens on a more abstract level and at a more accelerated pace through the process of credit transactions.

A credit transaction is an agreement to loan either goods or claims on unconsumed goods (money) to another person or group in return for repayment, usually plus interest, after the passage of some period. The exchange is based on the lender's confidence in the borrower's ability to pay out of future production. If the borrower makes good on his loan, he exercises his borrowed claims but also produces enough new wealth to replace them with claims of greater value. The positive difference between the value borrowed and the value returned is the lender's return for not consuming now.

If the borrower defaults, what happens is that the claims for the goods are exercised, the products are at least partially consumed, and not enough new wealth is produced to replace them. The creditor is left with the burden of redeeming what value remains of the debtor's holdings. The difference in market value between what is loaned and what is redeemed is a loss-wealth is consumed-the goods no longer exist in their formerly marketable form.

A credit exchange is neither a gift nor a grant; it is a trade just like any other on the market. The borrower, whether an individual or a group, earns and builds credit by consistently producing and meeting obligations undertaken in exchange agreements. The money may be borrowed for investment or consumption, but either way, the exchange is money or goods for a promise to pay. The lender chooses to loan the money rather than consuming it himself or investing it in his own pursuits, and in so doing puts confidence in the borrower's ability to repay.

The transaction is one based on a difference in time-preference between the creditor and the debtor. The lender, more precisely the depositor of savings, chooses to delay investment or consumption on his own account until some later date, and the borrower wishes to consume or invest beyond his current means and pay out of future production.

In a complex market economy, the majority of economic transactions involve credit of one form or another. Merchants receive their products from wholesalers with 30 days or longer to make payment. Auto dealers borrow money to buy inventory based on their ability to sell it profitably. Corporations borrow money through bond issues to finance business expansion. Stock speculators buy on margin. But no matter what form credit takes, it represents a claim on unconsumed goods traded by one party in return for a promise to pay by another. The lender chooses to forgo consumption until some future date, and the borrower chooses to consume now and pay for his consumption in the future.

I have already touched on the fact that when a bank makes a loan it doesn't lend away savings, it creates new money. Nevertheless, it does put actual savings (in the form of capital) at risk. On the upside, borrowers create enough new wealth to pay back the loan and still profit or at least break even. But on the downside, if they default, then existing goods are either consumed or rendered useless. When a business borrows money to invest in new equipment or machinery, two things happen: The business commits a portion of future profits to savings, and the lending institution puts actual savings at risk. In this way, no matter what the government's fiscal and monetary policy is, credit is tied directly to savings.

If I seem to be overemphasizing the fact that when you borrow money, what you are borrowing is someone else's claim on unconsumed goods, then it is only because I have been faced countless times by people who don't understand the relationship of savings, credit, investment, and wealth. Savings provide the basis for the extension of credit. Credit provides the fuel which accelerates investment in capital goods. And the accumulation of capital goods accelerates the rate of growth of wealth. But anytime a loan is "written off," someone somehow, now or later, pays the full price out of savings; that is, goods are consumed but not replaced.

There is a widespread and very dangerous misconception that because the government and the banking system can create money from what seems like nothing, they can also clean the slate of bad loans with an eraser without paying the price for real goods and services. The Treasury, in particular, is viewed as an unlimited resource, bound only by public confidence. And like the "unsinkable' Titanic, the sick irony is that the government is floundering from the continuing demands of special interest groups for handouts when, by ordinary standards of prudence, the treasury should be considered bankrupt.

There is nothing magic about government borrowing and government "guaranteed" notes and loans. When the government sells a bond or T-bill, the purchaser refrains from consuming and lets the government consume in return for a promise to pay in the future. But unlike commercial borrowing, the government's ability to repay is backed not by its capacity to produce in the future, but by its ability to tax in the future; which means that government borrowing is incurred at the expense of your and your children's future real income-their productive ability.

Government income, whether generated from taxes, borrowing, or inflation of the money supply is by its nature a burden on the productive capacity of the nation. It is a forced redistribution of wealth that shifts the balance of normal market factors. Most government activity is inherently consumption oriented and does not produce anything. 18

The fact that government lending and borrowing are "guaranteed" changes nothing. The guarantee is based solely on the ability to tax and print money. And if a debt is paid by printing money, the result is a debasement of the dollar's value through inflation, which is simply another (and much more perverse) form of taxation. You can't get something for nothing, but you can get nothing from something. Sooner or later, the debt incurred by deficit financing of government expenditures has to be paid in full, and so does the cost of a business expansion built and dependent upon easy credit. Whether the price takes the form of higher taxes, inflation, a general business decline (recession or depression), or some combination of the three, the price is always the same-wealth is consumed.

America never ceases to amaze me. I have a digital sender in my office that cost about $1000 and about once a week I marvel at what it can do. Somehow images on paper are turned to electric impulses that can be transferred over miles of cable to another machine where they are turned back into the same images.

I'm entirely ignorant about chips, digitizers, transducers, and so forth, but for a mere $1000 1 can reap the benefits of the creative minds and the countless hours and dollars that went into research, development, and marketing of that product. And I'm sure that if I had waited, I could have gotten a better product even cheaper.

On a simpler level, I can eat two eggs with toast and juice, and if I cook it myself, it costs me less than a dollar. Just think what it would cost if I tried to produce the same breakfast by growing wheat, grinding the flour, cultivating the yeast, raising the orange trees, raising the chickens, and so forth. It is simply fantastic-the closest thing there is to a free breakfast.

It's fantastic, but it is not an accident or a miracle; it is the result of productive people trading property by free association in the marketplace. Without government intervention, our economy would experience natural minor cyclical adjustments as the markets changed to accommodate new technologies, changes in consumer preferences, and shifts in credit; but production and prosperity would maintain an ever-increasing upward trend. But we have, and always have had government intervention. As a result, we have a business cycle subject to significant swings, both up and down. Everybody loves the upside, but very few know how to protect themselves from the downside.

As a businessman, the only way I know to protect myself from financial disaster in crashes, recessions, or depressions is through the ability to anticipate long-term market turning points and position myself accordingly. This means being leveraged and long at market bottoms and liquid and short at market tops. To do this requires an understanding of the basic economic principles I have described and the principles discussed in previous chapters.

In this chapter, I have presented the basic economic concepts required to understand the effects of government intervention on the markets. In the next two chapters, 1'11 show how the government, through deficit spending and the Federal Reserve System, intervenes with monetary and fiscal policy; and I will demonstrate how this intervention is the key determinant of the long-term trend of the economy. The objective is to show how to apply the fundamental principles of economics to stop the interventionists from consuming your capital while making money in the process.

Rally and Crash: Who Holds the Pump and Who Holds the Needle?

The wavelike movement affecting the economic system, the recurrence of periods of boom which are followed by periods of depression (recession), is the unavoidable outcome of the attempts, repeated again and again, to lower the gross market rate of interest by means of credit expansion. There is no means of avoiding the final collapse of a boom expansion brought about by credit expansion. The alternative is only whether the crisis should come sooner as the result of a voluntary abandonment of further credit expansion, or later as a final and total catastrophe of the currency system involved.¹

-Ludwig von Mises

RALLY AND CRASH: THE BUSINESS CYCLE

Since the mid to late eighteenth century, the debate has raged as to what causes large cyclical fluctuations in the market economy. In the context of this book. I want to answer that question so you can make money, not only during market upswings but also in the downswings when many businesspeople and most investors are losing money or are at least giving back a large part of previous gains.

I started this chapter with the quote from von Mises because I have never read a more accurate and well-formulated answer to the question of what causes the business cycle than his. In spite of his rather obtuse style, his reply is simple. But like Einstein's simple formulation, $E = mc2$, there is a lot of knowledge underlying the statement.

If you can understand the content of von Mises' statement with all its subtleties and apply it to the U.S. and world system of money and credit, you will be better equipped to foresee major market turning points than, say, 90% of speculators in the markets. In the statement, von Mises implies that to understand the business cycle; you have to understand the relationship of money, interest, credit, and the effects of credit expansion on the economy.

THE NATURE OF THE BUSINESS CYCLE

Almost everyone knows the kind of pyramid schemes such as Amway, and most of us don't participate in them because we rightly assume that either the founders of the schemes are crooked or that there is a good chance of ending up at the top of the pyramid with everything to lose and nothing to gain. The business cycle is like an incredibly elaborate pyramid scheme that repeats itself over and over again, introduced not necessarily by intention, but through widely accepted errors in economic thinking.

The phenomenon known as the business cycle didn't begin until the middle of the eighteenth century. Before that, there were depressions, but their causes were easily discernable. A king would need money to wage war or just to fill his purses and would send out his marshals to confiscate money (taxes). Naturally, this would cause a slump in commerce because it deprived people of their ability to carry on "business as usual."

Or perhaps during the war, one nation would deprive another of an essential resource, the way the North deprived Britain of cotton during the American Civil War, and cause a slump in industries dependent on that item, leading to a general economic decline. Whatever the source, it was relatively easy to identify the event which caused the economic downturn. Without these external, or exogenous, events, business went along in more or less a straight line with steady but moderate growth.

Starting in about 1750, however, there emerged a recurring cyclical fluctuation in the economic activity of industrialized nations that wasn't so easy to explain. There were two contemporary developments during this period of history: the industrial revolution, which began in England and spread throughout the western world; and the rise of central banking, specifically, central fractional reserve banking controlled by government regulators. Since these were the only new significant economic developments, political economists began to explore the possibility that one or the other of these two factors were responsible for the business cycle.

Two basic schools of thought emerged. One group, the mercantilists, assumed that there was something inherent, or endogenous, in the market economy which caused cyclical fluctuations in business activity. For this group, their focus was to find these reasons and then use government control to eliminate them and provide a stable environment for business expansion. The other group, led by the classical economist, David Ricardo, explained the business cycle by analysis of the effects of paper money and credit expansion on trade. In their terms, the business cycle is caused by the exogenous factor of government intervention in the money and credit markets. Unfortunately, the endogenous school triumphed, culminating in the economics of John Maynard Keynes, which in variant forms still dominates world economic thought today. Consequently, central banks, operating on the fractional reserve system, exist in every major industrial nation in the world-and so do booms and busts.

I realize that it is not enough to say that because central banks exist and booms and busts exist, that central banksters are the cause. But before I explain exactly how central bank expansion of money and credit creates the rally/crash cycle, let me give an example from history, an example which repeats over and over again, just with different players.

Although the business cycle didn't develop until the mid-eighteenth century, central banking began in 1692 with the foundation of the Bank of England. Almost simultaneously, in The Royal Commonwealth of Massachusetts, the first fiat money was issued (money with no redeemable value in the precious metals). Apparently, even this early in banking history, some government advisors had recognized the short-term benefits of credit expansion and fractional reserve banking. Perhaps the best illustration of this is the so-called Mississippi Scheme, which occurred in France in the early eighteenth century.

During his long and lavish reign from 1643 to 1715, King Louis XIV put the finances and economy of France into total disarray. After a period of prosperity brought about by extravagant royal spending, by the time of Louis XIV's death in 1715, both domestic and foreign commerce was on the decline, and the solvency of the French government was in question.

The national debt was 3 billion livres, the tax revenue was 145 million, and the state budget was 143 million, excluding the interest on the outstanding 3 billion debt. There was a debate whether the government should just declare bankruptcy and start from scratch, but the politicians of the time feared revolution and looked instead for a more expedient solution.

The government's first feeble attempt to remedy the problem was to devaluate the currency through a re-coinage, depreciating the currency by 20%. New coins were issued weighing 4/5 of the old coin, but with the same face value, and the populace was ordered by law to make the exchange. The net effect was to bring 72 million livres into the state treasury and to throw the commerce of the nation into a state of further disarray and economic depression.

To calm the public outcry which arose in response to the devaluation, the government slightly cut taxes and launched a reform program to eliminate widespread corruption among tax collectors. These measures drew public attention away from the crisis state of the country's finances but did little to bring the government into a state of solvency.

There emerged onto this scene a wandering Scotsman named John Law. An avid gambler and ladies' man, Law, had fled from Scotland to the European continent after killing a man in a duel over a woman. In Europe, he found a home for both his gambling skills and his twentieth-century ideas about money, credit, and government finance. Law was a firm believer that an entirely metallic currency system, unaided by paper money, was inadequate for the commercial needs of a country and limited economic growth. In other words, like John Maynard Keynes, Law believed that prosperity could be bought through carefully managed credit expansion and inflation of the currency.

Law lobbied the Duke of Orleans, his friend and the Regent of France,' and convinced him of the need for a private central bank to employ his currency and credit theories and bring France back to the fore as an economic power.

In 1716, the regent issued a royal edict authorizing Law and his brother to establish a bank, under the name of Law and Company, to be capitalized through the sale of 12,000 shares at 500 livres each, purchasable one-fourth in specie and the remainder in billets d'etat. The regent authorized Law's bank to issue bank notes instead of the coin and decreed the notes as acceptable, at full face value, for payment of taxes.

Law was no neophyte to banking. The son of a Scottish banker and an avid student of money, credit, and trade, Law knew that he had to establish public confidence in his bank's notes for the entire scheme to work. He immediately announced that all notes from his bank were payable on sight in the coin current at the time of issue. The public, reasonably fearing further devaluation of the coin, naturally favored holding Law's bank notes to coin and, almost immediately, the notes sold at a premium to the precious metals.

Public confidence in Law and his bank notes grew rapidly, the notes trading as high as a 15% premium to the metal coin, and branch bank offices were opened in five major French financial centers. During the same period, the billets d'etat were trading at a discount of 78.5% or more.

At this point, one could reasonably argue that Law's actions were based on sound economic principles. Above all, what France needed at the time was to restore confidence in the currency and credit of the nation. Law's fully backed paper currency did just that.

In effect, he offered his depositors an insurance policy against a devaluation of the coin. As long as people believed in the credibility of Law's bank and his ability to redeem his notes in specie, his notes were literally "as good as gold." With confidence restored in the currency, both foreign and domestic commerce enjoyed a resurgence. Taxes were paid with greater regularity, and the debt of the nation was gradually being retired.

But the Duke of Orleans, who didn't understand what was happening, thought that paper currency was the magic cure for all of France's economic woes. Seeing what he thought was an opportunity to retire the overwhelming government debt quickly, the regent made two fatal errors in 1717.

First, he authorized Law to form a company with exclusive trading privileges in the Louisiana Territory along the entire west bank of the Mississippi River, which was thought to be rich with deposits of gold and silver. The company was capitalized through the sale of 200,000 shares with a par value of 500 livres each, which could be purchased with billets d'etat at face value, even though they were trading at roughly 16% of their original value at the time.

Second, the regent made Law's bank public, declaring it the Royal Bank of France. Blind to the consequences of his policies, the Duke then caused, over a period of a few years, the issue of over one billion livres in paper currency. Whether Law agreed with this policy is not known, but when the bank was operating under his authority, the paper issue had never exceeded 60 million livres.

A billion livres weren't just handed out on street corners throughout France; they were given out as loans. In other words, there was a massive and rapid credit expansion resulting in an inflation of the paper currency. Also, in a further attempt to retire the still outstanding billets d'etat, another recoinage was ordered in which 5000 livres of a new and smaller coin were exchanged for 4000 of the old coins plus 1000 livres in the billets d'etat at their full face value.

The immediate consequence of the credit expansion was a speculative boom. Businesses and merchants that borrowed money bought domestic and foreign goods, domestic production was expanded, imports increased, and construction picked up. Leading the way in this boom was Law's Mississippi Company. The Duke of Orleans granted the company the exclusive rights to trade in India, China, and the South Seas, and to all the possessions of the French East India Company. The name of the company was changed to The Company of the Indies, and Law promptly arranged the sale of 50,000 new shares at 500 livres per share to be bought 100% with billets d'etat at their nominal value, while promising a 200-livre per year dividend to all stockholders.

There was an immediate speculative frenzy for the new stock issue. Believing Law to be a financial miracle worker, thousands of people filled the streets outside Law's residence, trying to get shares of the stock that was increasing in value daily. The Regent saw an opportunity to retire the entire remaining national debt and authorized another issue of 300,000 shares to be sold at 5000 livres each, again payable in billets d'etat.

You might think that such an enormous increase in the stock issue would have quelled the frenzied speculation. It didn't. The credit expansion simply fanned the fire and soon the price of the stock was rising as much as 10 or 20% in the course of a few hours. Stableboys and housemaids became wealthy overnight, and the general sentiment was that the magical source of prosperity would never end. Amazingly, the paper currency maintained its integrity for several years, but slowly and steadily, the gold and silver which supposedly backed the paper began to drain out of France into foreign countries.

As with all credit driven booms, the paper inflation caused prices in France to increase, making foreign products cheap relative to domestic products. As imports increased, special payments to foreign governments also increased, creating a drain on the nation's stock of gold and silver. Also, people who knew that gold and silver reserves at the Royal Bank were but a fraction of the paper circulation quietly began converting paper to coin and transporting the coin to foreign banks. By 1720, the scarcity of coin was so great that it was becoming impossible to carry out foreign trade, which was made with hard currency. To stop the run on gold and silver, the coin was decreed depreciated first to 5% below, and then to 10% below the paper, and special payments at the bank were limited to 100 livres in gold and 10 in silver.

These stopgap measures held back the coming storm until Law made a fatal error in February of 1720. At his suggestion, a decree was issued forbidding anyone to hold more than 500 livres in coin, and also prohibiting people from buying up precious stones, jewelry, silver settings, and so forth, under penalty of a heavy fine and confiscation of the holdings. The decree encouraged the public to inform on lawbreakers by providing an incentive reward of one-half the recovered amount. Rather than restore public confidence in the paper currency, this measure destroyed it and brought the country to the brink of revolution.

By May 27, 1720, the bank was forced to stop making payments in special, and the price of Law's stock was tumbling. The bubble burst, and the pyramid fell in what I believe was the first recorded stock crash in history. The stock of the India Company plummeted, and the value of the paper currency depreciated relative to gold and silver in spite of every effort by the government to achieve the opposite. Commerce was in total disarray, and every measure the government took aggravated and prolonged the problem. Law, once a national hero recognized as the savior of the glory of France, became the scapegoat for the entire problem and was nearly murdered by angry crowds. He eventually left the country, carrying with him virtually nothing of the vast fortune he had amassed.

A council was formed to restore order to France's financial system. Their audit found that rather than being diminished, the government debt had risen to 3.1 billion livres. The corruption they found within the government financial offices was unbelievable, and some of the guilty were sentenced to life imprisonment at the Bastille. Eventually, order and solvency were restored to some degree, but as history shows, the same mistakes were repeated, again and again, contributing to the impoverishment of the people and the growing division between the landed aristocracy and the working man. Eventually, these and other problems led to the abortive French Revolution and the eventual reign of Napoleon.

This story is such an excellent microcosm of the effects of credit expansion on an economy that I couldn't help but tell it. Every boom/bust cycle in market history follows a similar, but not as dramatic or condensed, pattern. The pattern goes something like this. After a period of economic decline-a bust-economic activity is sluggish and there is a social clamor for the government to "do something." While the market is in the process of a necessary adjustment, some ingenious economic guru links up with the government and offers a plan for recovery.

Invariably, the plan calls for an end to inflation, a balancing of the budget, decreasing deficits, and stabilization of the currency relative to foreign currencies. BUT (and there always is a but), the policies to achieve these noble ends always involve some form of interference in the workings of the free market and eventually amount to little more than a new credit expansion that results, sooner or later, in another boom and bust cycle.

Why does central bank credit expansion necessarily cause a boom/bust cycle? Simply put, it results in a misallocation of resources and confuses economic calculation to such a degree that either, like a drug addict, higher and higher doses of credit expansion are required to stay one step ahead of the inevitable consequences, or the economy goes into cold turkey-a recession or depression. But to fully understand what happens, you have to go back to the economic fundamentals; you have to understand the effect that credit expansion has on original interest.

Recall from the last chapter that Von Mises defined original interest as the ratio of the valuation of present goods to the valuation of future goods, or "the discount of future goods as against present goods." 5 It is original interest, as expressed by individuals exchanging in the marketplace, that determines the level of spending on consumer goods versus the level of capital savings. In other words, original interest determines how much of the available supply of goods in the marketplace is to be devoted to immediate consumption versus provisioning for the future. Its expression in the market is a component of the market rate of interest.

The market rate of interest tends toward the level of original interest held by a predominance of market participants. It is important to realize, however, that in the continuing operation of the market there is no fixed, constant level of original interest. Rather, it varies from person to person, market to market, and within each market according to changes in valuations brought about by changing conditions and opinions. But there is a tendency, caused by the competition of entrepreneurs, to drive original interest to a uniform level.

To understand how credit expansion causes the boom/bust cycle, you have to understand the distinction between original interest and the gross market rate of interest. The gross market rate of interest has three components: original interest, an entrepreneurial component, and a price premium. The entrepreneurial component is the portion of interest which gives the creditor incentive to lend money for investment. In effect, the entrepreneurial component entitles the creditor to a portion of profits gained through the investment of his money. The price premium is an allowance, either positive or negative, for anticipated changes in the purchasing power of money. To put it in somewhat oversimplified terms, original interest is the subjective value that the market places in consuming now versus consuming later, the entrepreneurial component is a premium which varies according to the creditor's confidence in getting his returns, and the price premium varies according to the lender's assessment of the purchasing power of money in the future versus the present.

All three components of the gross market rate of interest operate in every credit transaction; they are all always changing, and they all affect one another. As with any other market, the final determinant of the nominal interest rate on each loan is supply and demand. In a free market, entrepreneurs and promoters attempt to make profits by selling products at a price exceeding production costs plus the gross market interest rate. The role of the gross market rate of interest is to show entrepreneurs and promoters how far they can go in withholding the factors of production from immediate consumption for the purpose of creating more products in the future. The market rate of interest guides entrepreneurs to make the best use of the limited amount of capital goods available, which are provided by the savings of market participants.

Credit expansion by central banks, under certain conditions, can completely reverse this role. Assume for the moment that the credit expansion takes the form of making more money available for banks to lend, as happened in France during the Mississippi Scheme fiasco. In cases like this, money has a driving force of its own, and the loan market is directly affected before any changes occur in the prices of commodities and labor.

At first, no change in original interest occurs, but the entrepreneurial component of the gross market rate of interest rate drops due to the apparent availability of new capital for investment.

Although no additional capital does exist, when entrepreneurs put pencil to paper, the increase in the supply of money available makes it appear that it does exist. Previously unfeasible projects now seem to be feasible. In the early stages of a credit expansion, there is no way for the entrepreneur to distinguish between the money available and capital available-the the whole basis for economic calculation is distorted.

Artificially lowering the market rate of interest has no real relationship to the supply of capital goods available or the current level of original interest. But because of the distortion of increased credit availability, decisions are made as if they were directly related. As a result, capital goods are diverted away from their best use, encouraging poor investments and eventual capital consumption.

Also, the role of the price premium component of interest rates in the economic calculation is subverted. Because the money supply expansion directly affects the loan market before it affects prices, there is a lag time before the price premium can reflect the inevitable rise in prices which will occur as a result of the money supply expansion. Consequently, the price premium component of the gross market rate of interest is artificially low in the early stages of the credit expansion and creditors unknowingly make loans at too low an interest rate.6

In a fractional reserve banking system? Credit expansion always causes inflation in the money supply, as I will discuss in detail shortly. Advocates of an inflationary expansion argue that the price increases which occur from money supply increase affect commodities before they affect wage rates. Consequently, they say, producers' costs go up, consumer prices go up, and the wage earners and salaried people, who have less tendency and ability to save than other classes in the market, are forced to restrict expenditures, and savings are made available for capital expansion.

On the other hand, they say, entrepreneurs and businesses, who have a greater tendency to save, enjoy the benefits of higher prices and increase their savings in more significant proportion than consumption. As a result, there is a general trend toward an intensified accumulation of new capital paid for by the diminished use of wage earners and salaried people. This forced savings lowers the rate of original interest and therefore, because of an increase in capital investment, accelerates the pace of economic progress and technological innovation.

While this may be true at times, and indeed has happened at certain times in the past, it is an argument that overlooks several important facts. First, it is not necessarily true that wage rates always lag commodity prices. Labor unions in the 70s, for example, caught on to the effects of inflation and bargained for real increases in salaries above and beyond the rise in the Consumer Price Index (CPI)-the so-called "wage-price spiral." There is also no guarantee that entrepreneurs and businesses will always necessarily save more than wage earners and salaried people. But perhaps the most important fact that this argument overlooks is that inflation introduces forces in the market that tend toward capital consumption.

Inflation-an increase in the money supply caused by central bank credit expansion falsifies economic calculation and accounting. When the central bank makes a greater amount of money available on the credit market, it makes additional loans available that otherwise would not have been. The simple interest rate-the actual average percentage interest rate-might not change, but because more money is available in the credit market, the gross market rate of interest is lowered. Consequently, loans are made that would not have been made before the expansion. This is exactly what the Fed is trying to accomplish now.

To entrepreneurs, who deal and think only in dollar terms, the availability of credit makes formerly unfeasible projects appear feasible. For them, credit is a claim on unconsumed goods to be invested in new projects. As more and more entrepreneurs embark on new projects, business activities are stimulated, and a boom begins. But there is an inherent problem from the outset of the boom. At any point in time, the goods and labor available for business expansion are finite, or scarce. The increased demand for these rare items caused by the credit expansion creates a tendency for a rise in the prices of producers' goods and the rates of wages.

With the increase in wage rates, there is a corresponding increase in demand for consumer goods, and their price begins to rise as well. This happens in stages, affecting different sectors of the economy at different times and to different extents. For many businesses, rising prices of their products on the consumer market give the false appearance of real gains on their accounting ledgers. Encouraged by these illusory gains, these businesses calculate that they can now afford to consume more, and they too contribute to the rising prices of consumer goods. Producers' prices are affected first and the most dramatically, but the rising prices of consumers' goods reassure the businessmen that their capital expansion program will pay for itself in spite of the rising costs of production.

Von Mises was the first economist to realize how this whole process occurs. It gets a little bit complicated here, but I urge you to stick with this analysis because understanding it will help you avoid losing money by being fully invested at bull market tops.

In Von Mises' terms, call p a number of capital goods available on the eve of credit expansion, r the replacement capital which must be saved from the gross proceeds of production with p, and g the total amount of consumer goods that are produced from p. Further, assume that the economic condition prior to the credit expansion was a progressive one that produced surplus capital (capital savings) of p, and p2 which, without the advent of the credit expansion, would have been employed to produce the incremental quantity g I of goods produced previously and the quantity 92 of newly developed goods.

Without the credit expansion, the result would be that p (the existing capital) would produce r + g (the necessary replacement capital plus the goods that p produced for consumption) and capital savings of p1 + p2 (new capital to increase existing production plus capital to invest in new projects). Growth would come from using pi + p2 to produce g1 + 92 (more existing products plus new products), and technological innovation would accelerate the process. But instead of this happening, the central bank, trying to stimulate employment and production, puts money into the system creating additional credit availability.

Enticed by the credit expansion, entrepreneurs decide to produce an additional quantity, 93, of goods previously produced, and embark on new ventures designed to create 94 of newly developed products. To produce 93 and 94, additional capital goods, p3 and p4, are needed. But as I already mentioned, the capital available for business expansion is limited to p, and p2; p3 and p4 don't even exist, they just seem to! The entrepreneurial decision to produce 93 and 94 is based on an illusion brought about by the credit expansion.

Looked at this way, the actual quantity of capital goods at the disposal of entrepreneurs for planning is p, + p2 + r, but the apparent capital available is p I + p2 + p3 + p4 + r. Entrepreneurs act as if they could produce g I + g z + 93 + 94 with the apparent capital available and, because of the lack of real capital available, a bidding war ensues for p1 + p2 + r. Prices for producers' goods rise and may, at first, outstrip the rise in consumers' goods prices, causing originary interest to decline in the near term.

During this period, the increased interest in producing for the future may actually bring about the generation of real new wealth. But eventually, as the credit expansion continues, the rise in prices of consumers' goods outstrips that for producers' goods. The rise in wages and profits (largely apparent, not real) intensifies the demand for consumers' goods before the capital is in place to provide them. Consumer prices rise. If consumer prices continue to rise, eventually people want to own consumer goods as soon as possible to avoid paying more for them in the future. In other words, there is a tendency to raise originary interest, which means there is a tendency toward increased consumption in the immediate term versus provisioning for the future. Capital, in the form of savings, is consumed. This often reaches the point where people like Donald Trump will borrow as much as possible to own items which they believe will cost more or be worth more in dollar terms in the near future. From an arithmetic standpoint, interest rates may rise as a result of the increased demand for loans. But the entrepreneurial and price premium components of the interest rate necessarily lag behind what is required for the "proper" allocation of capital. Banks assume that their higher rates are enough to compensate for the effects of changing prices, so they continue loaning to businessmen, confident that the business expansion will continue indefinitely.

In fact, however, their confidence is a false one because they fail to realize that they are fanning the flames of the bidding war for scarce capital. As entrepreneurs, judging that they can meet the increased costs of production through increased sales, continue to borrow money to expand production, interest rates continue to rise, as do the prices of both producers' and consumers' goods. Only by a continued increase in the supply of money created by the banks can the boom continue.

But soon, even that is not enough. If banks continue their expansionist policies, eventually the public becomes aware of what is happening. They see that the real purchasing power of their money is on the decline and a flight to real goods begins-the originary interest in holding goods skyrockets and that of holding money plummets. It is at this stage that runaway inflation, such as that which until recently existed in Brazil and still exists in Argentina and other nations, takes hold. Von Mises calls this stage of credit expansion a "crack-up boom."

Normally, however, things never go quite this far. Consumers on fixed incomes cry to politicians about the rising cost of living. Politicians blame someone else and urge the central bank to put on the brakes. The central bank responds by restricting credit availability. Entrepreneurs, unable to afford the now scarce loans, abandon new projects as they realize that they are doomed to failure. Banks stop lending because they realize that they have already overextended themselves. Loans are called in. The monetary expansion stops.

At this, the turning point of the boom, prices begin to fall as businessmen, hungry for cash to service their debt, sell off inventories. In particular, the price of producers' goods usually falls precipitously and to a greater extent than consumers' goods, such as in 1929 to 1933, when retail sales dropped 15% while the sales of capital goods dropped about 90%. Factories close. Workers are laid off. And as confidence in the economy wanes, the entrepreneurial component of interest rates jumps to excessive heights which further accelerates the deflationary process. Accompanying this process is usually some kind of news which turns the already existing crisis into a panic, often reflected in a plunge of stock and commodity futures prices. The bust occurs.

Typically, after such a crash, economists decry the failure of capitalism and declare that "overinvestment" was the cause of the bust. This is a huge mistake and the most misunderstood aspect of the boom/bust cycle. It is not overinvestment, but what Von Mises calls "malinvestment" that causes both the boom and the bust. It is the fact that lowering the gross market rate of interest through credit expansion encourages entrepreneurs to attempt to employ $p_1 + pZ + r$ (the actual capital) as if it were $p_1 + p2 + p3 + p4 + r$ (the apparent capital) that causes the problem. It necessarily brings about investment and distribution of resources that is out of whack with the real available supply of capital goods.

It is like trying to build the foundation for a 5000 square foot house out of concrete sufficient for a 2500 square foot house-either you alter the plans or you spread the concrete so thin that it won't support the structure.

As I discussed in the last chapter, to increase wealth requires the savings of surpluses for investment in future production. Technological innovation accelerates the rate of growth of wealth but is possible only through the application of saved capital. Most often, during a credit expansion, part of $p_1 + p2 + r$ is invested in innovations which accelerate the real rate of growth of wealth, offsetting some of the negative effects described above. But this is only a damper.

The nature of the distorted investments brought about by the credit expansion must sooner or later collapse, and wealth will be consumed. It may be true, and most often is, that by the end of the boom/bust cycle, the actual standard of living and overall wealth in the economy is greater than at the beginning. But it is certainly not greater than it would have been during the same period without the irresponsible credit expansion.

As a speculator participating in markets influenced by credit regulation by central banks, you must be able to identify the stages of the boom/bust cycle. To do this, you have to understand the different forms that credit expansions take. Specifically, you have to understand how both the Federal Reserve Board and the Treasury contribute to money and credit inflation. Since central banks in all nations operate in basically the same way, once you understand how the U.S. system works, you will have a grasp of how all central banks work. Then, you will have the basis to understand and potentially to predict the economic outcome of politicians' attempts to coordinate both national and international monetary policy.

THE STRUCTURE AND ROLE OF THE FEDERAL RESERVE SYSTEM

In the title of this chapter, I posed the rhetorical question: "Who holds the pump, and who holds the needle?" In France during the Mississippi Scheme, the answer was John Law and the Duke of Orleans. In the United States today, the parallel answer is the The Federal Reserve Board and the Federal Open Market Committee

(FOMC). These organizations monopolistically control the supply of money and credit in the entire Federal Reserve System which now includes, de facto, nearly all depository institutions in the country.

The economic power that they wield is absolutely mind boggling. It is so great that we have become a nation of Fed watchers, clinging to the obtuse proclamations made by the Fed Chairman and other key Board and FOMC members as we look for some indication of forthcoming policy. A single statement made by the Fed Chairman can literally reverse the stock market trend, as happened on July 24, 1984, when then Chairman Paul Volcker announced, "The Fed's [restrictive] policy was inappropriate." That same day, the stock market made its low, and a new bull Ironically, an agency which can literally swing the market with a sentence was established by the Federal Reserve Act of 1913 to stabilize the workings of the money and credit markets.

In the words of the legislation, the purpose of the Federal Reserve is to "give the country an elastic currency, to provide facilities for discounting commercial paper, and to improve the supervision of banking." By 1963, the Fed's acknowledged objectives had expanded "to help counteract inflationary and deflationary movements, and to share in creating conditions favorable to a sustained, high level of employment, a stable dollar, growth of the country, and a rising level of consumption."g (Note the emphasis not on production but on consumption-pure Keynesianism.)

158

Today, the Fed is virtually another branch of government which attempts to coordinate its policies with Congress, the President and the Treasury, and the central banks of foreign governments. But the primary function of the Fed is to act as the central bank of the United States. Let's first look at its operation in this role.

As the nation's central bank, the primary function of the Federal Reserve is to:

... regulate the flow of bank credit and money. Essential to the performance of this main function is the supplemental one of collecting and interpreting information bearing on economic and credit conditions. A further function is to examine and supervise State banks.... obtain reports of condition from them, and cooperate with other supervisory authorities in the development and administration of policies 9

The Fed's big stick is its power "to regulate the flow of bank credit and money," which means, plain and simple, to inflate or deflate the supply of money and credit.

Before I go on, let me briefly define what "the Fed" is. The Federal Reserve System has three basic components: the Board of Governors, the Federal Open Market Committee (FOMC), and the Federal Reserve Banks. As an agency of the Federal government, the organization of The Federal Reserve System is mandated by law, but little else is. The Board and the FOMC-the seven board members occupy seven of the twelve seats on the FOMCunilaterally establish and implement the monetary policy of the United States. It is these two components that people generally refer to when they use the words, "The Fed."

The Board consists of seven Presidentially selected appointees, confirmed by the Senate, who serve 14-year terms. The terms are arranged such that one expires every even-numbered year, and a member may not be reappointed after serving a full term. The Federal Open Market Committee consists of the seven Board members plus five presidents from the twelve Federal Reserve District banks, one of whom is always the president from the New York Bank. The other four members serve one-year terms which rotate among the other 11 district banks.

The FOMC is responsible for establishing and implementing the monetary policy of the United States. While the Board has unilateral control over the discount rate and reserve requirements (within bounds prescribed by law), it attempts to set its policies according to objectives established by majority vote at FOMC meetings. The meetings are currently held eight times per year. The committee decides its own schedule and ad hoc meetings may be called at any time. In addition, the FOMC decides upon a plan of open market operations to attempt to achieve its policy objectives, and the plan is carried out by the Federal Reserve Bank of New York. Open market operations consist of buying and selling of government securities by the Fed on the open market. These transactions have an immediate and direct impact on the reserves held by the banking system and therefore on the availability of credit and the rate of growth of the money supply. It is through this process that the Fed expands or contracts credit availability and manipulates interest rates. Let me explain this process in detail.

HOW MONEY AND CREDIT AVAILABILITY IS CREATED AND CONTROLLED

In the last chapter, I described how in the early stages of banking history, lenders discovered that they could issue more gold- or silver-backed bank notes than their actual holdings of gold and silver. As long as the public had confidence in the institution's ability to redeem the bank notes in coin on demand, then the bank could create paper money, or fiduciary media, which was acceptable in the marketplace as a medium of exchange. I also showed, through the description of the Mississippi Scheme, the disastrous results which can come from pushing this process too far price inflation and ultimate economic collapse.

The basic principles are the same in The Federal Reserve System, with one huge exception-there is nothing backing the dollar except a government law declaring it to be legal tender. This is called a fiat money system. The value of the dollar is totally dependent on the market's faith and confidence in its purchasing power, which is ultimately determined by the supply of and demand for currency in relation to other goods and services available in the market.

As a substitute for precious metals, which were used to serve as one of the checks of paper money expansion, the Fed establishes reserve requirements which, since the passage of The Monetary Control Act of 1980, must be adhered to by all depository institutions in the United States.[10]

Reserve requirements are a percentage of reserve liabilities that must be held by depository institutions in the form of reserve assets. Reserve liabilities consist of transaction deposits, time and savings deposits, and net liabilities to foreign banking offices (Eurodollar liabilities). Reserve assets consist of vault cash (actual dollars and coin) held by the depository institution and reserve deposits held at the Federal Reserve District Banks. In essence, reserve requirements act as the depository institution's only objective check on credit expansion, and therefore on the expansion of the money supply.

For example, if a commercial bank has transaction deposits (deposits with unlimited checking privileges such as checking and NOW accounts) of $100 million,

Table 10.1 Reserve Ratios, May 1990

Type of liability	Reserve ratio (%)
Transaction accounts	
$0-40.4 million	3
More than $40.4 million	12
Time and savings deposits	
Personal	0
Nonpersonal, by maturity	
Less than 1½ years	3
1½ years or more	0

Net liabilities to foreign banking offices. (Eurocurrency liabilities) 3 it must currently have at least $12 million in vault cash and/or deposits at the Federal Reserve Bank in its district. The $100 million is the reserve liability and the $12 million is the reserve requirement as calculated according to the current reserve ratios established by the Board of Governors (see Table 10.1).

In terms of money creation, there is an inverse relationship between reserve ratios and the amount of money a depository institution can create. For example, a reserve ratio of 10% means that for every dollar of added reserve assets in the system, 10 dollars of new money can be created. In more realistic terms, if the Fed buys government securities of $250 million in a week, with a reserve ratio of 10% this creates a potential for $2.5 billion increase in the money supply. Conversely. the sale of $250 million in securities creates a potential contraction of $2.5 billion in credit availability.

This is difficult to see if you try to think in terms of all depository institutions, their transactions on the market, and their transactions with the Fed District Banks. But it is relatively easy to see if you look at a model of a hypothetical country; let's call it Newmoney, with a Central Bank and a fractional reserve system.

I'm going to take you through the credit expansion process step by step, and show you how the Fed, or any Central Bank, can literally create or destroy money at the stroke of a pen. For simplicity, I'm going to show only the affected portion of the balance sheets, so don't look for a balance between assets and liabilities. On a complete balance sheet, obviously, both sides would balance.

Assume for simplicity that the only kind of deposits in the Newmoney are demand deposits (checking accounts), that there is a total of $1 billion in those accounts-all as loans-and that the central bank has established a 10% reserve ratio. Also assume that the banking system in Newmoney stays loaned up to the maximum allowed by the central bank. Then, the relevant portions of the consolidated balance sheet of the Newmoney Central Bank and the consolidated balance sheet of all depository institutions in Newmoney would look something like this:

Simplified segment of the consolidated balance sheet of the Newmoney Central BankRelevant Assets (thousands of dollars) Government securities 150,000

Relevant Liabilities

Newmoney Central Bank Notes 100,000 Reserve Deposits 95,000

Simplified segment of the consolidated balance sheet of all Newmoney depository institutions

Key Assets (thousands of dollars)

Loans 1,000,000

Vault cash 5,000

Reserve Deposits at Central Bank 95,000 Government and other securities 150,000

Key Liabilities

Demand Deposits 1,000,000

Notice that the combined reserve assets of commercial banks (vault cash plus reserve deposits at the central bank) of the depository institutions equal exactly 10% of their reserve liabilities (10% of demand deposits). At this point, the bank's hands are tied. No new loans can be made because the loans would become demand deposits and put the banking system in violation of the 10% reserve requirement.

But let's assume that the Board of the Central Bank meets and decides that the unemployment rate is too high in New money and that to stimulate new business and new jobs, they want to increase the availability of credit.

To do this, they engage in open market operations and purchase New money government bonds from the banks to the tune of

$50 million. When they buy these securities, they write checks against themselves (out of thin air) that the banks then deposit in their reserve accounts at the Central Bank. The transaction occurs with nothing but ink.

The banking system as a whole now has $50 million more reserve deposits. So now their balance sheets look like this:

Simplified segment of the consolidated balance sheet of the New money Central Bank

Relevant Assets (thousands of dollars) Government securities 200,000

Relevant Liabilities

New money Central Bank Notes 100,000 Reserve Deposits 145,000

Simplified segment of the consolidated balance sheet of all New money depository institutions

Key Assets (thousands of dollars)

Loans 1,000,000

Vault cash 5,000

Reserve Deposits at the Central Bank 145,000 Government and other securities 100,000

Key Liabilities

Demand Deposits 1,000,000

Now the banks have excess reserves of $50 million; that is, they have $50 million more on deposit with the Central Bank than they need to meet the 10% reserve requirement for existing demand deposits. That means they have enough excess reserves to support another $500 million in loans ($50 million divided by 10% equals $500 million). Being generous and patriotic men that want to see full employment and economic growth, the bankers promptly approve all sorts of new loans.

When the banks make the loans, they create an asset and a liability which automatically balances on their ledgers. In this case, when the $500 million in loans are made, the banks credit the borrowers' demand deposit accounts by $500 million and credit their asset sides with loans so that the affected portion of the consolidated balance sheet now looks like this:

Simplified segment of the consolidated balance sheet of all Newmoney depository institutions

Key Assets (thousands of dollars)

Loans 1,500,000

Vault cash 5,000

Reserve Deposits at Fed District Banks 145,000 Government and other securities 100,000

Key Liabilities

Demand Deposits 1,500,000

So, by purchasing securities on the open market worth $50 million, the central bank set a chain of events in motion that increased the money supply by $500 million-$500 million of new money was created. The exact reverse would happen if the central bank sold securities in open market operations.

I want everyone who is reading this to understand that this is a simplified version of what actually occurs, not only with the Federal Reserve System, but with every central banking system in the world. The actual workings are more complex; but I could show in a more detailed discussion how, no matter how many banks are involved, the potential impact on the supply of money and credit is virtually identical to what I just described in the hypothetical country of Newmoney. For you doubters out there, it's a good mental exercise.

In net effect, when the Fed purchases securities, it creates, on paper, the money with which it buys those securities-it simply writes a check on itself. That new money, in turn, enters the banking system and may be used to increase reserve assets held by the banking system. The increase in reserves assets creates the potential for an increase in the money supply through credit expansion equivalent to the reserve increase divided by the net average reserve ratio. When you leave Newmoney and enter the real world, things then start to get a little more complicated.

If you look back at Table 10.1, you will see that reserve ratios in the Federal Reserve System currently vary from 0 to 12% depending on the type of liability. If you buy a 10-year, $10,000 certificate of deposit from your bank for cash which has been stuffed in your mattress, the reserve ratio is 0 for that item (it is a time deposit with over 1 y2 years to maturity), and the banking system as a whole can potentially expand its loans by $10,000/.12, or $83,000! When the Fed buys securities, the exact same thing can happen.

The net reserve ratio-an equivalent ratio which would give you required reserves for deposits as a whole-depends on where the market chooses to place its money. But to give you an idea of the relationship of required reserves to depository liabilities as a whole, the data in the May 7, 1990, issue of Barron's shows the broadest measure of the money supply, M3, at $4.066 trillion, while total reserves deposited in Federal Reserve District banks equalled only $60.3 billion. Of that 4 trillion plus number, actual currency equaled only $228.4 billion, which means that the rest consists of deposits (liabilities) in accounts of one form or another at various institutions.

So the ratio of reserve assets to monetary deposits as a whole is almost 1 to 70. Even assuming that M3 is not an accurate measure of the total money supply, the same issue of Barron's reported that the Fed then held $233,966,000 in government securities. Assuming a net average reserve ratio of 10%, that gives the 12 men who make up the FOMC the power to add over

$2.3 trillion in potential credit availability to the system-over half of M3!

Are you beginning to understand why open market operations are such a powerful tool of monetary policy?

Plato, the Greek philosopher, believed that the common man was incapable of governing his own life and affairs. Ideally, he thought that philosopher kings should rule the world. In a sense, Plato got his wish. The members of the FOMC are the philosopher kings of the U.S. economy, and as the sovereigns of the most powerful industrial nation on earth, they wield enormous power over the world economy as a whole. They are the kings, and the markets are the subjects-free to act only within the confines of sovereign dictate.

Just 12 men on the FOMC-the members of the board and five district bank presidents-vote to set policies which critically constrain and alter free market action. They set objectives in terms of and take action based upon broad, aggregate economic statistics such as unemployment figures, capacity utilization, the Consumer Price Index (CPI), the Producer Price Index (PPI), the growth and rate of growth of the money supply (as measured by MI, M2, and M3), the trade balance figures, indices of the money supply (MI, M2, and M3), reserve balances, and many other indicators. They constantly monitor these macro indicators and alter their strategy-in secret at the FOMC meetings-according to what they agree. by consensus, is needed to better achieve their policy objectives.

Now I've simply got to put in an aside here. When the FOMC meets, they purposefully withhold their decisions from the market. Yet, the 12 members of the committee all bring aides to the meeting. Most of the committee members are married and have families, as are most of the aides. In addition, secretaries and staff must type up and duplicate the minutes. Now, in a country where the National Security Council can't sneeze without the press getting wind of it (no pun intended), do you really think the decisions in the meeting stay completely a secret? I don't. And in fact, that gives me an idea.

Instead of raising taxes and doling out welfare, why doesn't the government secretly distribute the minutes of the FOMC immediately after the meeting to committees responsible for the development of depressed areas of the country. They could train these committees to trade in the markets and use the secret knowledge to get a jump on the rest of us who trade government securities. You could virtually end poverty in depressed areas! Of course, I'm not serious, but in my opinion, a select few are getting the jump anyway!

Who holds the pump and who holds the needle? Without a doubt, the Fed does, in the form of Open Market Operations and the other policy weapons available to them to control the supply of and demand for money and credit. In order of increasing importance, the Fed has three principle tools of monetary policy: setting reserve requirements, setting the discount rate, and performing open market operations.

As a speculator, you need to understand the nature of these tools and how the Fed uses them in order to accurately assess the likely direction of future market movements. Let me discuss each of these weapons in turn.

RESERVE REQUIREMENTS, FED FUNDS RATE, AND THE DISCOUNT RATE

In terms of the mechanical workings of reserve requirements, little more needs to be said than what I brought out in my discussion of the New money banking system. But it is important to understand the different ways banks can achieve their reserve requirements and how the Fed uses its hand within this context both to affect the supply of money and credit and to monitor the activity of lending institutions.

The Board uses reserve ratios to establish reserve requirements that can only be met by holding sufficient reserve assets-vault cash and deposits with the Federal Reserve District banks. Because money is constantly moving in and out of individual lending institutions, a particular institution may have a deficit or surplus of reserve assets in the short term. In the case of a deficit, a bank or lending institution has one of two choices: either it borrows the excess reserves of another institution on a short-term basis, or it can borrow from the discount window at the Federal Reserve bank in its district.

The market for borrowing the excess reserves of other institutions is known as the Fed Funds market, and the prevailing interest rate charged is known as the Fed Funds rate. This "borrowing from Peter to pay Paul" market and the interest rate which accompanies it is very important to watch. Although it is ostensibly designed to facilitate banks with a short-term reserve deficit, what it actually does is enable the system as a whole to stay loaned up to the fullest extent possible.

In fact, it is such an important market that until 1979 the Fed based its open market operations primarily upon trying to achieve a target Fed Funds rate, thinking that the interbank interest rate would determine the ease or tightness of borrowing for reserves, which would in turn set the standard for the credit market as a whole. But if you review the Carter years (197(-1980), you'll find near runaway inflation, followed by interest rate controls, followed by a credit crunch, followed by deregulation and 22% interest rates!

Obviously, targeting a particular level of the Fed Funds rate was a totally inadequate tool for controlling credit availability. Like any other item in the marketplace, supply and demand determines how much credit expansion will occur. In the Carter years, people willingly borrowed and banks willingly loaned money at high interest rates because they thought rates might go still higher. In late 1990, however, there were plenty of excess reserves in the system, but banks simply weren't making loans.

Until 1979, in addition to trying to control the Fed Funds rate, the Fed also attempted to use the discount rate as means to control credit expansion. The discount rate is the interest rate that the Federal Reserve District banks charge lending institutions for borrowing reserves directly from the central bank. In theory, the discount rate was supposed to be set by the board of each Fed District Bank, subject to review and approval by the Federal Reserve Board. In practice, however, the discount rate is now uniform throughout the system and is established by the Federal Reserve Board with District banks automatically approving the Board's "recommendation" as a formality.

There are several differences between the discount rate and the Fed Funds rate. First and foremost, discount window borrowing is inflation of the most blatant form. When a bank borrows from the discount window, the Fed writes a check against itself, creating money that then serves as new reserves for the borrowing bank.

The borrowing bank pays interest (the discount rate) on the borrowed reserves and the system as a whole is able to expand loans by approximately 10 times the amount borrowed. The discount rate is always lower than the market rate of interest so, just like I used to do when I started trading options, the borrowing bank "makes the middle" when it makes new loans secured by reserves borrowed through the discount window.

But there is a catch. Borrowing from the discount window flags the borrower as being possibly overextended. No one wants a federal agency breathing down its throat and monitoring its activities, so lending institutions are limited in the number of times they can go to the discount window. Basically, when they borrow from the discount window, they are given a silent, but not so subtle message, "Clean up your act, bad child, and provide the reserves you need from your own sources."

By comparison, the Fed Funds market is much more free. As long as banks can successfully "make the middle" and pay off their loans to fellow banks, they can borrow reserves in the Fed Funds market. During the late 70s, Fed credit was running amuck because the board was reluctant to sell enough securities to make the Fed Funds rate rise to a level that discouraged interbank borrowing for credit expansion.

It was all Volcker could do to get the Board to approve a ½-point raise from 10 ½ to 11 % in the discount rate (a 4 to 3 vote), much less encourage open market securities sales to increase the Fed Funds rate.

What the Fed failed to realize during the 70s is that interest rates aren't the sole determinant of the supply of and demand for money and credit. It goes right back to Von Mises' explanation of the three components of the gross market rate of interest and how they change during the boom/bust cycle.

If, during an expansionary period, originary interest is low because of rising prices, if the price of the premium component is perceived by the market as being a bargain because interest rates are continuing to rise, and if the entrepreneurial component (no matter how high interest rates are nominally) is perceived as surmountable in profit/loss calculations, then the markets will borrow as much money as they can!

In other words, no matter what the actual interest rate number is, if both the supply of and demand for credit exists, money will be loaned and the credit expansion will continue. Another reason the Fed couldn't quell the credit expansion of the 70s was that only Federal Reserve member banks were subject to reserve requirement restrictions. This meant that unregulated lending institutions could create money, which in turn ended up as new deposits in Fed member banks. Further fueling the credit expansion. In addition, the foreign liabilities (such as Eurodollars) of member banks and other institutions were exempt from the same reserve restrictions as domestic liabilities, and dollars created abroad were entering the system and further stimulating the growth in the money supply.

We were in the latter stages of a boom fueled by credit expansion, prices were rising in every sector, and the sentiment was that prices would continue to rise indefinitely. People were making paper fortunes in real estate, the commodities markets, stocks, you name it, and there was no end in sight; simultaneously, the average worker on fixed income was infuriated by the government's inability to put a lid on rising prices. It was Law's Mississippi

Scheme on a grand scale. Still, as long as interest rates were on the rise, a loan today was better than a loan tomorrow because the markets realized that the purchasing power of the dollar was declining. Politicians kept the pressure on the Fed to keep interest rates low so they could keep their constituents happy. Those in government who were aware of the dangers of what was happening were afraid to act for fear of collapsing the house of cards and ruining Democratic hopes for the next election.

By the last quarter of 1979, the U.S. economy was universally engaged in a flight to real goods. Gold skyrocketed in price, peaking at nearly $875 per ounce in the futures markets in early January 1980. Nobody wanted to hold paper money. Rather, they bought stocks, futures, real estate, or gold, held it for a year, or even a few months, and then turned it over for a 20% gain! Magic! Instant wealth! Doesn't this ring a bell-something like the Mississippi Scheme?

Fortunately, there was enough prevailing economic wisdom to realize that we were heading for a "crack up boom" similar to what existed in Germany in the 30s and what exists in some South American countries today. On Tuesday, October 12, 1979, Paul Volcker returned prematurely from an International Monetary Fund/World Bank meeting in Belgrade, Yugoslavia and announced an emergency meeting of the FOMC to take place on the following Saturday (The Fed likes to meet and make announcements at times when the markets can't react immediately to their pronouncements.)

At 6:00 PM. on that Saturday, Volcker convened a press conference in which he outlined a plan that would revolutionize the Fed's approach to monetary policy.

Volcker announced that the discount rate would be raised from 11 to 12% and that new, restrictive reserve requirements would be imposed on banks' foreign liabilities. Both actions demonstrated the Fed's resolve to bring inflation under control. But the real kicker was Volcker's proclamation that from then on, the FOMC would control the money supply directly by controlling reserves through open market operations rather than by shooting for target Fed Funds rates. At this point, Volcker was engaging in psychological tactics to cool the speculative fever. After the election in 1980, the real tightening would come.

My point in telling this whole story is to show that the philosopher kings really do control the economy and with very limited knowledge. The Fed has been experimenting with our economic lives by trial and error. But before I go into that aspect of the Fed, let me discuss open market operations in more detail.

Open Market Operations

Any open market operation-the purchase or sale of securities by the Fed-has a direct dollar for dollar influence on the amount of reserves available in the system; a purchase increases reserves, and a sale decreases reserves. If you understand how a gold-backed monetary system works, the Fed's power with open market operations is tantamount to the Fed sitting on millions of ounces of gold and injecting or removing it from the banking system at will-a power that would be considered monopolistic if wielded by the private sector.

There are several types of open market operations, and each has a slightly different effect on credit availability and monetary growth. Some operations are more hidden than others and some are very blatant. If you understand the different types and monitor the Fed's activities, you can not only get an idea of the direction of monetary policy, but even more important, you can gain insight into the psychology of the men on the Board and the FOMC. And since it is the minds of these men that largely determine the direction that economic activity will take, it is essential to understand the direction of their thinking.

There are two basic approaches to open market operations: long-term and short-term. For trying to achieve long term operating objectives, the primary tool is the outright purchase or sale of securities, usually U.S. Treasury issues of bills, notes, and bonds. If the objective is to increase reserve availability, the manager will purchase securities from dealers in an auction process until the desired amount of reserves are added. If the objective is to remove reserves, the manager will sell securities to dealers, again in an auction process. Another method of withdrawing reserves is to let securities held in the system's portfolio mature without replacement.

To compensate for short-term deficits in reserves caused by things such as increased seasonal demand for currency (as in the Christmas buying season) and other short-term technical factors, the Fed uses repurchase agreements (RPs), often called repos by the market. In a repurchase agreement, the Fed buys securities from dealers with the agreement that the dealers will buy them back within a specified period (the period can vary from 1 to 15 days but is usually 7) at a specified price, usually with the dealer having the option to terminate the agreement before maturity.

The flip side of repurchase agreements is matched sale purchase transactions. "Matched sales," as they are called, consist of a contract for an immediate sale of securities (usually T-bills), and a matching contract for purchasing the same amount of securities from the same dealer at a later date (usually not exceeding seven days). Matched sales are a way for the Fed to remove reserves from the system on a short-term basis in response to seasonal or other technical factors.

Described like this, these operations seem innocent, even reasonable. But at the risk of repeating myself, you need to be aware that all open market operations represent the creation or destruction of ink deposits in banking accounts. When additional reserves are created, the banking system has the capacity to increase the money supply by making new loans. In Von Mises' terms, the gross market rate of interest is lowered, regardless of the nominal level of interest rates.

Conversely, if reserves are pulled out of the system by the sale of securities, the banks will lose credits in their reserve accounts at the Federal Reserve Banks. If the contraction reduces reserves to such a level that lending institutions have a net deficit in reserves, loans will be called in, inventories will be reduced, and a business contraction will ensue-the gross market rate of interest is raised even if nominal interest rates remain unchanged.

Repos and matched sales, while short-term tools, can have a significant long term impact. If the Fed regularly engages in repos such that there is a consistent balance of securities held under repurchase agreements, then from the standpoint of the banking system as a whole, these balances are tantamount to outright purchases.

The Fed Funds market is very efficient. It is in any bank's interest to loan excess reserves, even if on an overnight basis. A continuous balance of reserves added to the system by repurchase agreements can have an important impact on the Fed Funds market and the Fed Funds rate. It is also significant if the Fed discontinues a regular policy of supplying short-term reserves through repos. This is a somewhat hidden way of tightening "a little bit." The converse is true for matched sales or changes in matched sales balances.

The most apparent and readable of all Fed policy actions are outright purchases and sales. The news wires report these immediately when they occur, and their effect is usually predictable.

Perhaps the best indicator of the effects of Fed policy, however, isn't the quantities of outright purchases and sales but the level and changes of the level of free reserves in the system.

Free reserves equal excess reserves minus discount window borrowings other than extended credit." This number, which is reported every Sunday in Barrons and other financial publications or can be obtained directly from the Fed. Is a key measure of the degree of ease or tightness of Fed policy. As an approximation, if the free reserve number is positive, then you can multiply the number by 10 to calculate the approximate current potential credit availability on the market. A negative number means that a credit contraction is in progress. But, the number doesn't have to be negative to indicate Fed tightening.

The Fed can tighten while maintaining a positive level of free reserves. It is helpful to think in terms of Von Mises' formulation of the gross market rate of interest. If the level of free reserves declines, then the gross market rate of interest increases, regardless of the nominal interest rate.

This means that less capital is apparently available for investment than before. The converse is true if the level of free reserves increases, other things being equal. To get the best reading, what you should look for is changes in levels of free reserves in conjunction with changes in the Fed Funds rate, the discount rate, the rate of growth or decline of the adjusted monetary base, 1= the rate of growth of the money supply, and the CPI and PPI numbers.

One thing you can count on is that, on balance and in the long term, Fed policy will be expansionary, the money supply will continue to expand, and the purchasing power of the dollar will continue to fall. According to the U.S. Department of Labor and the Bureau of Labor Statistics, what cost $1.20 in December 1988 cost only 30 cents in 1961 and only 10 cents in December 1913. But the Fed's expansionary monetary policy isn't the only reason that the dollar's value is diminishing. Our government's continuing policy of deficit spending is to blame as well, and it is important to recognize the impact that deficit spending has on the business cycle.

Deficit Spending and Its Effects on Money and Credit

Here are some hard facts. The last time the U.S. government didn't operate at a deficit was 1969, when it reported a surplus of approximately $4 billion. Since then, the trend has been toward an ever upward spiral of deficit spending so that the March 1990 deficit-the deficit for one month-was larger than that for the entire 1975 fiscal year.

According to Grant's Interest Rate Observer, at the end of fiscal 1989, gross federal debt totaled $2.866 trillion, not to mention the $4.124 trillion face value of government insurance programs, and the $1.558 trillion in outstanding federal credit. Government outlays in 1989 were 22.2% of GNP, and that was a seven year low! The interest expense on federal debt was 3.3% of GNP and hasn't been below 3% since 1983. As of September 30, 1988, the net worth of the country was estimated by the Comptroller General to be negative $2.4526 trillion, omitting public lands and mineral rights except at nominal values."

In large part, these numbers speak for themselves. The U.S. government is a debt junkie, and if the trend continues, the doses are eventually going to become lethal.

Suppose you have two credit cards. each from a different bank; and each month you pay the balance of one card by charging it to the other card, while simultaneously spending more than your paycheck each month. The respective banks, unaware of your practice, keep increasing your line of credit because you always pay in full-you're a good and valued customer in their eyes.

While the banks don't know what's happening, you start waking up in the middle of the night with anxiety attacks about the increased amount of interest you pay each month, wondering how long it will be before the scheme blows up in your face.

That's basically the way our government has been operating for the last several decades. It borrows money from two main sources: the public, or the Fed itself: and it borrows more money in each cycle to pay its debts.

If you listen to politicians talk about deficits and their impact on the value of the dollar and the business cycle, you'll be nothing but confused. The party out of power always blames deficits for chronic inflation, while the party in power declares that deficits have nothing to do with inflation.

Both statements are wrong. If the Treasury sells its bonds to the public to fund the deficit, money is transferred from the public's hands to the government's hands. The government then spends the money, putting it back into the public's hands, albeit redistributed. There is nothing inherently inflationary in this process-no new money is created as a direct result of the securities sale.

On the other hand, if the Treasury sells securities directly to the Fed, the money used to pay for them is "printed"-the Fed credits the Treasury's account with the purchase price of the bonds, plus it increases its inventory of securities for open market operations. This process is obviously, and directly inflationary, but it is not a common practice. But there is a more subtle way that deficit spending induces inflationary policies by the Fed.

If the government is a debt junkie, the Fed is the pusher providing the supply of the deadly substance-credit. It works something like this: If the government needs to sell $100 billion in government securities to the public (including the banking system itself), the Fed buys $10 billion of securities on the open market to enable the banking system to lend the $100 billion needed to finance the new Treasury issue.

It's a rich and self-fulfilling scam-no different in principle from the Mississippi Scheme. When the government operates this way, it guarantees a supply of credit for itself in the short term and financial trouble for all of us in the long term.

There are many mistaken notions which beset economic thinking about government debt. One of the biggest is that government deficit financing has no effect on credit availability in the private sector. To support this assertion, some analysts point to the 1982-83 period, when deficits were not only high but on the rise, while nominal interest rates fell.

In fact, a study I carried out in January 1983 shows a characteristic inverse relationship between deficits and nominal interest rates; interest rates virtually always drop during periods of high deficits and rise as deficits decrease. But this doesn't mean that deficits have no effect on credit availability. It is a huge mistake to equate low nominal interest rates with the real interest in borrowing money.

The main reason for the inverse relationship of interest rates and deficit spending is the policies of the Fed. During periods of recession, unemployment rises, businesses cut back production and borrow less, and profits diminish, with the net effect that government revenues decline. Simultaneously, the demand for government social services and guarantee programs increases because of economic hardship. Consequently, the level of government deficit spending increases during times of economic recession.

Acquiescing to anti-recessionary political pressures, the Fed then pumps money into the system by purchasing huge quantities of government securities on the open market, creating excess reserves and artificially driving down the gross market rate of interest. The low interest rates are a mere facade that mask the lack of real capital available for borrowing.

Nevertheless, the low nominal interest rates draw entrepreneurs in, and a stimulated recovery begins. As the recovery gains momentum and the level of borrowing picks up, the demand for credit increases relative to the supply, and interest rates begin to move up. Jobs are created, tax revenues increase, and the deficit, or at least its rate of growth, declines.

Another important impact deficit spending has on the credit markets is dictated by the law of supply and demand. The economic facts of the matter are that any time the government borrows money in the market, it is taking potential resources out of the private sector and putting them into the government sector.

Money borrowed is a claim on unconsumed goods, and at any point only a limited amount of unconsumed goods are available on the market. Therefore. When the government borrows money, it gains a claim on unconsumed goods that would otherwise be available to the private market. Nothing can change this simple fact. When the Fed pumps so much money into the credit market that interest rates remain unchanged or even drop in the face of massive government borrowing, it simply masks or waters down what is actually occurring-the artificial lowering of the market rate of interest, the distortion of economic calculation, and the misallocation of resources.

An historical example of this process began in 1969. The Fed reduced the rate of growth of the money supply, interest rates shot up, and the country went spiraling into recession. Credit demand faded, and interest rates began to decrease. Because tax revenues diminished and government spending increased, the budget figures moved from a surplus in 1969 to a deficit of $2.8 billion in 1970 to $23.4 billion in 1972!

The discount rate moved steadily downward from 6% in 1970 to 4.5% in 1971. Then the credit expansion began to have its expected impact. Business activity increased. Employment was stimulated. Company earnings began to improve. As a result, Federal tax revenues increased, and the deficit plummeted to $4.7 billion by 1974.

Consumer prices were also affected-they soared! The CPI (1982-1984 = 100) moved 10 full points from 35.6 in 1969 to 46.6 in 1974-over a 28°k increase in just five years!

Faced with rising consumer prices, the Fed once again put on the brakes and. once again, recession struck. From 1974 to 1976 the discount rate dropped from 8% to 5 1/4% while the deficit soared from $4.7 billion to $66.4 billion. And the cycle continues today.

Another prevailing fallacy is that tax increases are a cure for deficits. As Parkinson's Law states, "Expenditures rise to meet income." The net level of taxes has increased in every administration since the Kennedy administration, while deficits have grown to all-time highs. The only way to cut deficits is to cut the budget.

As if direct deficit spending isn't bad enough, there is another growing burden which James Grant calls "the latent deficit"-all the contingent liabilities and government guarantees accumulated since the New Deal. The face value of U.S. government insurance programs has grown from $662 billion in 1979 to $4.214 trillion in 1989. Direct loans, loan guarantees, and GSEs (Government Sponsored Enterprises) have grown from $200 billion in 1970 to $1.558 trillion in 1989.

To put some of these figures in more concrete terms, almost 75% of all farm loans are facilitated by the government, and approximately 88% of housing mortgages are federally supported by some means. 14

1 don't want to sound like a prophet of doom, but this process has to stop sooner or later. When it does, because of the huge scale of what has been happening, we are going to see the most severe economic correction-bust-in history, provided the government lets the correction run its course. But depending on how the Fed, the Executive, and Congress handle the problem, we could continue for a long time to come with spurts of stimulated economic growth followed by short, sharp recessions which slow down the expansionary, inflationary process.

As a speculator in this kind of economic climate, you have to be constantly aware of the downside possibilities. You have to carefully monitor Fed and Treasury activities and pronouncements and be prepared for the market's response.

HOW TO PREDICT THE TREND AND CHANGES OF TREND BASED ON FED AND TREASURY POLICY

Market forces-supply and demand-ultimately determine the long-term price trend of any market. But part of the supply and demand equation in any market is the supply and demand for money and credit. Whether you are trading stock indexes, individual stocks, or commodities, both Fed and government fiscal policies dramatically affect money and credit and therefore the price trend.

My biggest wins have come from the ability to predict the consequences of government policies (combined with other methods, of course). But my biggest losses came when I assumed that the government would behave rationally.

For example, in July 1982 I had one of the largest long positions of my life. We were in a bear market, and Dow Theory gave me a buy signal. I went long the world, and within three weeks was up $385,000.

But on July 23, Bob Dole came out with a tax bill proposing the largest tax increase in the history of the world. I made the mistake of believing Reagan's campaign promise not to raise taxes and assumed the bill would never pass. The market fell 12 out of the next 14 days, and by the time I got out of the position, my profit had turned into a loss. I posted a loss of over $93,000 for the month, the second largest losing month of my career. (Actually, the losses were about twice that; the $93,000 was just for Interstate.)

The market bottomed on August 12, when the news arrived on the market that the Fed would ease. The psychology of what happens in this kind of case is really amazing, if you think about it. The federal government, operating at a deficit, increases taxes at the tail end of a bear market to help alleviate the burden of deficits.

The Fed, fearing that the increased tax burden will drive the economy deeper into recession, realizes that the only way the tax bill will do any good is if business is stimulated into recovery, so they pump money into the system, which drives down interest rates, and business begins to expand. In essence, by expanding credit, the Fed provides the government with the resources to pay the bill of the new tax law. And people call this a free marker economy!

Another case where I lost money by believing in politicians occurred in November 1984, after Reagan's reelection. His proposed new tax law was presented as "simplified" and "revenue neutral." I believed him, and was long more than ever in my life-pages and pages of calls on stocks. It turned out that "revenue neutral" meant that the government was going to take money from corporations and give it to individuals, and the market went down nine of eleven days. I lost over 5349,000 that month, by far the largest monthly loss of my career, and, again, my actual total losses were almost double that.

My failure in these two cases was not thinking like a politician, but at least I learned something. I learned that you can count on politicians to take the expedient route, the "pragmatic approach," no matter what their expressed intentions are. I became almost cynical as I watched an avowed gold standard and laissezfair advocate, Alan Greenspan, take the chairmanship of the Federal Reserve Board and turn into an expert at saying nothing with far too many words-the hallmark of every "good" politician. I watched the federal budget grow and deficits soar under an administration that ran on a campaign of "limited government" and "a return to free market principles." I watched the economic bubble inflate, driven by the most rapid credit expansion in U.S. economic history. By mid-1987. I was poised, waiting for the needle that would pop the bubble, and the rest is history.

Make no mistake about it, the Fed is a political institution subject to the pressures of the lobbyists and constituencies of Congress and the President. Why`' It's the nature of the beast. Any man who tries to remain aloof from those pressures will lose both his influence and, eventually, his position. It is naive to expect the Fed to act as a truly "independent agency." In large part, the members of the Fed are forced to act on the basis of the short-term, pragmatic policies of the patty in power, not on the basis of sound economic policy. A trading rule that you won't see in the chapter on trading rules is: "Never go long politicians-and the Fed is a group of politicians."

Predicting the long-term trend based on government fiscal and monetary policy is basically a matter of thinking in fundamental economic principles in the context of the nature of the business cycle. The central problem is one of being vigilant and of assuming a politician's mindset when evaluating the pronouncements of the President, the Secretary of the Treasury, and key members of the Fed. There are really only two long-term possibilities-prices are going to trend up, or they are going to trend down. And the turning points will occur when the Fed changes its policies to accommodate government fiscal policy or to actively reverse a market downtrend. At the risk of being redundant, I will repeat the Von Mises quote I used at the beginning of this chapter. By this time, the meaning should be more clear:

The wavelike movement affecting the economic system, the recurrence of periods of boom which are followed by periods of depression [recession], is the unavoidable outcome of the attempts, repeated again and again, to lower the gross market rate of interest by means of credit expansion. There is no means of avoiding the final collapse of a boom expansion brought about by credit expansion. The alternative is only whether the crisis should come sooner as the result of a voluntary abandonment of further credit expansion, or later as a final and total catastrophe of the currency system involved.

CONCLUSION

In this chapter, we have seen that the business cycle is the result of credit expansions and contractions, induced by government fiat, and controlled in monopolistic fashion by the Federal Reserve and the fiscal policy makers in government. We have also seen that as long as the government controls monetary policy, there will be booms and busts. And as long as there are booms and busts, there will be an opportunity for the speculator to make money both on the upside and the downside. It is ironic that as an advocate of a purely free market, most of my knowledge would become obsolete if the Fed were put out of business and we went on the gold standard. But, unfortunately, I don't see that happening, at least not in my lifetime.

As long as government induces these cyclical fluctuations by manipulating the money and credit markets, it is the speculator's job to profit from it. By monitoring both government policy and the policy makers, you can often anticipate their actions and therefore predict the economic consequences. It all goes back to what I spoke about in the first chapter-thinking in principles.

When Fed policies and government fiscal policies fly in the face of basic economic principles, draw conclusions based on the fundamental economic principles involved, and you'll be right. The problem from there is one of timing-timing how long it will take the markets to recognize and react to the effects of faulty government policy. And that's where knowledge of Dow Theory, technical methods, and all of the essentials I've talked about so far-come into play.

Chapter 7
Managing Money by Measuring Risk

THE REAL MEANING OF RISK

Suppose I told you that it is possible to measure risk in the stock market objectively. For those of you who are pros, I know what you're thinking: but just hear me out. Now, assume that you were long the stock market as of October 9. 1989, and I told you that the odds were then better than seven to one that the market would fail. If you had known these odds and believed them, would you have changed your investment strategy at all? If you were long at that point, I think you would have.

The fact is that there is a way to measure risk in the stock market in quantitative terms; there is a way to determine the probability of the market going up x% versus going down y%. It's not a "system"; it is a consistent method of gauging the likelihood that the current market trend will continue or fail. It is an approach that allows a speculator or investor to change his or her primary focus from the determination of "value," which is subjective and always changing to objective risk.

But what is risk? When I started my career on Wall Street, I knew a lot more about playing poker than about the markets, but I also knew that there were many similarities. Both require skill and luck, but more skill than luck. Both require knowing how to manage money so that even if you lose a few hands, you'll still be around to play in the next one. And both involve exposure to the chance of losing money, which is the meaning of risk.

In my late teens, instead of making minimum wage bagging groceries. I made a decent income playing poker. I was good at poker because I knew how to measure and manage risk in the game. Instead of focusing on the size of the pot I only stayed in when the odds were in my favor: my focus was on the risk involved if I stayed in. Risk involves chance, and chance involves odds. Odds take two forms: either those set subjectively by a professional oddsmaker or those that are measurable according to probabilities based on a statistical distribution of limited possibilities.

In poker, odds are measurable, concrete, and objective. For example, assume you are sitting on the right side of the dealer in a game of five-card draw poker with five players. With a $10 ante, there is $50 in the pot after the first round. If the first player bets $10 and everyone has called but you, then there is $90 at stake in the game-your potential reward is 9 to 1. Assuming that you have four hearts and want to draw for a flush (the chances of a flush being a winning hand are a minimum of 1.0037 to 1), your chances are 1 in 5.2 that you will draw another heart-your risk is 5.2 to 1. With a risk of 5.2 to 1 and a reward of 9 to 1, the risk/reward for the current round is 1.73 to 1 in your favor. With a risk/reward of 1.73 and a probability of .9963 that a flush will win, the adjusted/risk reward is 1.73 x .9963, or better than 1.72 to 1 in your favor.

If you employ this kind of strategy consistently, you may lose individual hands. You may even have a bad run of luck now and then, but you will win much more money than you lose over the long haul. I don't consider this gambling. Gambling is taking a blind risk. Speculation is taking a risk when the odds are in your favor. That is the essential difference between gambling and speculation.

Naturally, because my focus on risk had worked so well for me in cards, when I came to Wall Street I sought a method of objectively defining the odds of being right or wrong when speculating in the stock market. But when I asked pros whom I respected how they determined risk, I got chuckles and comments like, "You can't measure risk in the markets. It's not like cards. It's not a mathematical business. The market is a random walk game," or "The efficient markets theory invalidates risk/reward analysis."

Instead of talking about measuring risk, they spoke about distributing risk, or even more often focused on "values," saying things like "Find value, buy value and hold it, and you'll do well over the long term." This advice went against my grain: I didn't want risk exposure unless I could objective and determine that the odds were in my favor.

The advice of market professionals is more sophisticated today than it was in the past 20 or 30 years, but it is not substantially or predominantly different. Most experts today think in terms of distributing financial resources according to some relative measure of performance or value. For example, Alpha and Beta are typical tools used in stock portfolio management. Alpha is a measure of quality which compares the performance of an individual stock relative to the market. An Alpha value of 1 means that the stock has, on average, outperformed the market by 1 % per month, so if the market moves up 10% in six months, that stock should move up 16%. Beta is a measure of volatility. A stock with a Beta of 2 should be up 20% when the market is up 10%, or down 20% if the market is down 10%.

Most money managers buy stocks according to some set Alpha and Beta combination, plus other relative factors such as price to earnings ratios, book value, and yields; and they call this "risk evaluation." But think about it. What do these measurements have to do with risk? What do they tell you about the current trend of the economy or the effects of a change in Federal Reserve policy? What do they tell you about the likelihood that the market as a whole might be subject to a sustained and dramatic decline? The answer is: "not much!"

I am by no means implying that these measures are worthless, far from it. But to use them as primary tools in speculation or investment assumes that value is an objective, static concept. Value implies evaluation, which means that individual human minds determine it. What something is worth depends totally on what people in the marketplace decide it is worth. Value can change and often does rapidly. Consider the case of Penn Central.

In early 1970, Value Line Investment Service announced that the company was "worth" $110/share (as measured by the value of its underlying assets) and that it was "undervalued" at $74/share. By this measure, the stock price should have soared. It went to $2/share! The analysts who calculated the value of the company's holdings failed to take account of the fact that those holdings would deflate in value during a recession. They assumed that the market's standard of valuation would remain unchanged.

More recently, in 1990, some analysts were saying that Citibank was "undervalued" at $24 1/2. What they assumed was that Citibank was too big to fail, that there wouldn't be a recession, and that therefore Citibank's previously bad loans would turn into good loans. All of their conclusions rested on the assumption of this occurring, and did not take into account the risk of a market downturn.

In a market downturn, the Citibanks, the Trumps, and any entity that is highly leveraged against assets that depend on dollar appreciation through continued inflation are subject to decline and possible failure.

Now consider the concept of buying and holding "value." The problem with this view is that there is only one true measure of value, and that is the market. For example, IBM has been a standard for such "value." But if you bought "Big Blue" in January 1983 or later and held it until November 1989, then you would have been losing money during the third largest upward stock market movement in this century! Why "hold value" by being invested in a declining stock? Why experience all that pain when you could have made money instead?

The problem with the conventional approaches to market involvement is that none of them address one straightforward and fundamental question: "What are the odds that the current market trend will continue?" In other words, what is the risk of being long or short in the current market? Alpha, Beta, value, yield, PEs, book value-all of these measures have merit, but only as secondary considerations when you have a firm grip on the most likely direction the market trend will go. What is first necessary is a primary standard to gauge the risk of market involvement in general. So, how do you measure the risk of being long or short in the stock market?

A REVOLUTIONARY APPROACH TO RISK ASSESSMENT

Answering this question eluded me for several years. To measure something, you have to identify a quantitative relationship established by comparison to a standard unit reference value. In the financial markets, this presents a perplexing problem: How do you set a standard to measure risk and determine the probability of success without being arbitrary and subjective in the process?

Markets aren't like a deck of cards with a limited number of permutations possible; they are composed of individuals engaged in the pursuit of their own unique set of desires or values that are by their nature subjective-unique to the situation and frame of mind of each person. So it would seem that to gauge market behavior accurately, to predict the likelihood of success of any investment, you would have to be practically omniscient and be able to read every person's mind simultaneously and be certain how they would react to coming events. It is impossible to predict the future of price movements with absolute certainty. The best we can do is deal in probabilities, so the question becomes: By what standard do you measure probabilities in the financial markets?

Any time you speak in probabilities, you are speaking of the odds of something occurring based on a statistical distribution of possibilities. Insurance companies use statistical data, such as mortality tables, to set insurance premiums. For example, the current odds of a 24-year-old white female dying in New York are 50,000 to 1. The average life insurance premium for a $100,000 policy for this group is $100 per year. According to the statistical odds, the probable outcome is that the insurance companies will gross $500,000 in premium payments for every $10,000 they pay out to the beneficiaries of 24-year-old white females who have died. That is odds of 50 to 1 in the insurance company's favor. Not bad odds management. It is no wonder that most well-managed insurance companies are so profitable (the ones that didn't fill their balance sheets with junk bonds and real estate).

There is nothing certain about the life expectancy of anyone individual, but that doesn't mean it is impossible to define a standard with which to gauge the odds of a single person living to a certain age within a given standard of health-insurance companies make such measures their business. The same type of reasoning can be applied to the stock market. In 2002, I began a two-year, intensive study of stock market movements dating back to 1986, which I still keep current to this day. What I found is those market movements, like people, have statistically significant "life expectancy" profiles that can be used as the standard for the measurement of risk exposure. Let me explain.

After I missed the October lows in 2002, I started asking myself some questions so I wouldn't make the same mistake again, questions like: "What exactly is a trend? How high or low does it usually go? How long does it usually last?" Drawing on Charles Dow's identification of the three concurrent market trends-the short term, lasting from days to weeks; the intermediate term, lasting from weeks to months; and the long term, lasting from months to years-I went back in history and classified every price movement in the Dow Jones Industrials and Transportation (Rails) averages, logging their extent and duration in statistical distribution tables.

Using Robert Rhea's classification methods, I identified primary movements, intermediate primary movements, intermediate secondary corrections, plus some other less important classifications. The result was a set of statistically significant bell curve distributions for the extent and duration of all market movements since 1896.

In a bell curve distribution, statistical samples tend to bunch around the median or midpoint of the distribution. For example, the current median extent for bull market primary intermediate swings on the Dow is 20%. Of the 112 bull market primary swings since 1896, 57 of them, or 50.89%, have reached an extent of between 15% and 30%, while the minimum move was 4.3% and the maximum was 116.6%. Twenty-five percent of the moves went to highs above 30%, and 33.04% of the moves failed below 15%. Based on these criteria alone, you would be wise to bet that a primary swing would appreciate somewhere between 15% and 30%. But of course, you would never use these criteria alone.

Think about how life insurance companies go about gathering their information. The first question they ask is age. Then they factor in job hazards, medical history, family history, and so forth. But the mortality tables are the standard of reference, the starting point of evaluating the risk of insuring the customer. In the same way, I use my distributions as a means to establish the base probability that a market movement will reach or go beyond a given extent and duration. I do not use them to predict the exact levels the current market movement will reach or how long it will last! Market turning points occur when the tide of market participants' judgments changes. This is usually driven by fundamental economic factors, the policies of the Federal Reserve Board, major world events, and so forth, as I discussed in the last chapter.

To use extent and duration profiles to predict in advance exact market turning points would be like having an insurance company tell you when and how you will die on the day you buy your policy. I don't mean to be morbid, but just as each individual person dies in a different manner, context, and point in time, so markets die. But who are you most likely to see on stage next year, Billy Idol or Bill Murray? What these profiles do is tell you is the base probability, in the context of history, that the current stock market trend will continue or fail.

Returning to the insurance analogy, if two men, one 18 years old and one 75 years old, both in good health, went into an insurance company to apply for a term life policy, then the younger man would pay a very low premium, and the older man would pay a very high premium. The premiums would be set such that the risk, according to the statistics, of the person dying before he pays the entire policy value plus interest is very low. But if the older man had a temperature of 102 and were a heavy smoker, he wouldn't be sold a policy at all.

Consider the examples of the October 1987 crash and the 2007 crash in a similar context. The primary intermediate movement leading to the crash of 1987 began on 5/20/87. By 8/25/87, the Industrials had increased 22.9% in 96 days, while the Transports had increased 21.3% in 108 days. These were nearly the exact median levels, both in extent and duration, of all bull market intermediate movements in history. In life insurance terms, the market had reached the median life expectancy, meaning that 50% of all middle movements in history ended before this one was a likely candidate for retirement. From this standpoint alone, caution was warranted, so it was time to examine the medical history.

The market was no Arnold Schwarzenegger. There were divergences; the Dow made a new high in August, but the advance/decline ratio did not-a bearish indication. PEs were at an average of 21 times earnings, the highest levels since 1960's when they were at 22. The average book value to price ratio was nominally higher than 1920's. The government, corporate, and consumer debt were at unprecedented levels and all the rest that

I've discussed before. In October 1987, the market was not only no Arnold, but it was also an alcoholic, with pneumonia that smoked three packs of unfiltered Camels a day.

Consequently, smart investors were out of the market and looking for an opportunity to short it. The first sign was in October when the Wall Street Journal read: "Fed Chairman Greenspan said interest rates could become `dangerously high' if inflation worries 'mushroom' in financial markets. Greenspan called such concerns unwarranted but hinted the discount rate might have to rise to allay them." The next day, stock prices plunged a record 91.55 points for no immediately apparent reason other than Greenspan's pronouncement. On October 15, Dow Theory gave a sell signal and traders went short thinking that the patient's heart could fail with even the slightest excitement.

The heart attack occurred when Germany and Japan failed to heed James Baker's request to stimulate their economies (inflate) to protect the value of the dollar. In response, Baker announced to the world on Sunday, October 18, that he "would let the dollar slide." Traders knew at this point that the financial markets would collapse from the dollar devaluation. When the market gapped down on October 19, Traders shorted the opening of the S&P 500 futures and made a substantial profit for their account in that position alone.

The point in describing the thinking before the crash of October 1987 is to show how watching extent and duration criteria can clue you into the potential health of the market. They act as a caveat telling you to pay close attention to what is happening fundamentally. Sometimes they say more than that. For example, Many professionals were essentially out of the market from May until October of 1989; because they feared the downside possibilities. By 10/9/89 the net appreciation primary intermediate up move on the Dow, which began on 3/23/89, was 24.4%. During the same period, the Transports had moved 52%, fueled by takeover stocks. Let me put this into the framework of my statistical base. The median net appreciation, or yield (the net percentage move if you buy and hold from the bottom of one intermediate correction to the next), for primary intermediate movements (primary swings) in bull markets, is 10%. Further, only 15 of 112 such moves in history yielded more than 24.4% (the gain that was current in the existing primary swing as of October 9). Even more important. Only 8 of 174 upward movements in both bull and bear markets had matched or exceeded the Transport's 52% gain. In other words, the odds, based on history, that the market would fail ranged from 7.46/1 to 21.75/1! That told traders to close any longs and look for a shorting opportunity. Measured by statistical criteria alone, to be long in October 1989 was one of the poorest risks on record. And once again, the fundamental and technical factors were on the side of the statistics.

The new high set by the Industrials on October 9 was unconfirmed by the Transportsa bearish indication. As of Friday, October 13, the Japanese and the Germans had raised interest rates, making it more expensive for their companies and citizens to buy American products on credit. The Fed had reduced the money supply and credit availability (as measured by free reserves) over the previous two reporting periods, and with the CPI already at an annual rate of approximately 5.5%, they did not have much room to ease to stimulate business activity, which was already sluggish. Northeastern real estate and the regional banks holding the mortgages were already in recession. The bottom had already fallen out of the junk bond market. In short, the patient was once again old and sick, and another stroke was imminent-not a good time to write an insurance policy at any premium rate. It was certainly no time to be long. Some were fortunate to be short at the right time and in the right instruments, but it was statistical profiles that clued them into the downside possibilities.

Anybody who knows me knows that I don't mind playing the short side. But I want to emphasize that this approach to risk assessment is equally valuable to pension fund managers, who must be long to some extent in the stock market. Suppose the fund manager is trying to determine what percentage of capital to allocate to the stock market, with 60 being an aggressive position and 20% being the minimum allowable position according to the investment charter of the fund. If the stock market is in the third primary swing of a bull market, then the statistics say that the median extent and duration for third primary swings are 139 days and 18.8% respectively. If the market had appreciated 12% in 103 days, the manager would know from the profiles that 16 of the 23 third primary movements in bull markets had lasted longer. On that basis alone, the manager should commit no more than 69% of the maximum 60% to stocks. In other words, by the statistics alone, they should commit a maximum of 41.4% of the portfolio to stocks.

I want to emphasize again that this is only a starting point, a basis from which to evaluate the risk of market involvement. If under these same statistical circumstances, inflation was at 1%, PEs were at nine, interest rates were at 5%, and earnings were soaring, then the manager would underweight the statistics and invest the full 60% in stocks.

This concept of risk measurement has been instrumental to my success in the markets, particularly in positions involving either long-term or intermediate-term market turning points. It allows me to place my primary focus on risk, which is the basis of my approach to speculation. But no matter how you make market calls or stock selections, market life expectancy profiles provide an objective base context within which to gauge the risk of market involvement. They add a unique and powerful new dimension to risk assessment.

ALLOCATING CAPITAL WITH ODDS MANAGEMENT

As mentioned in Chapter 2, my primary focus is to minimize risk, while simultaneously putting enough money in the right place to make consistent profits. What it takes to do this is a prudent system of money management.

Money management is the art of allocating financial resources and timing entry and exit to and from the marketplace to achieve business goals. A reliable approach to money management must consist of three crucial components: (1) a method of assessing risk/reward, (2) a means with which to determine the probability of success on any given trade (whether short-term, intermediate-term or long-term), and (3) a system of asset allocation. And, since you are dealing with money, these three components must, at least predominantly, be reduced to objective, measurable criteria.

I have already discussed my statistical profiles and how I use them to measure risk. Also, if you recall, I pointed out that my risk/reward criterion is at most 1 to 3, and I demonstrated how I determine that ratio technically on the charts. It amounts to looking at the chart, evaluating where you think the market can probably go-the target point, establishing the point where the market proves that you are wrong, and determining your exit point, and then calculating the following ratio:

This ratio expresses technical risk/reward in terms of maximum probable losses versus probable potential profits. Properly considered, risk/reward from any dimension is always a ratio of probabilities. Where it gets tricky is in establishing a way to quantify probabilities when dealing with other than technical factors. When assessing risk/reward, a whole range of information, including both technical and fundamental economic principles, comes into play. Let me illustrate how to combine these factors by examining a position my father took in gold in October 1989.

He bought gold on 10/27/89, the day the market confirmed a 1-2-3 change of trend in the intermediate term by breaking above the previous rally high of 376.70. At this point, there was also a probable change of the long-term trend by the same criteria-both the break in the trend line (condition 1) and the test and failure of the previous low (condition 2) had already occurred.

In the intermediate term, because he had a confirmed change of trend, the market would prove him wrong if prices fell back through the buy spot, so he set his mental stop slightly below that point, at 375.70. The target point in the intermediate term was the 7/25/89 high of 399.50. So his technical risk/reward ratio was:

376.70 - 375.70 = 1

399.50 - 376.90 22.6

When he looked at the long-term chart (the weekly bar chart), things looked even better in terms of the potential levels gold might reach. There, he could see a target price (resistance) at 433.50. After that, there was another resistance point at 469.50, one at 502.30, and if he looked at an even longer-term chart (at a monthly bar chart), he saw prices in the 800 range. I won't bother calculating the risk/reward of each point for you, but you can see that the ratios were extremely favorable.

From a technical standpoint, trades this obviously good don't come along too often. The only problem is to figure out the probability of success and establish your entry and exit points. What do you do: Play the intermediate term, or buy and hold for the long term?

To help answer this question, what he did was to assume the most conservative case. That is since the intermediate trend had already changed by definition, he assumed that this would be an intermediate trend lasting from three weeks to three months. Next, he went back in history to 1981 and tabulated the extent of every upward move in gold lasting from three weeks to three months.

He found that, of 18 such moves, the minimum movement was 9.4%, the maximum movement was 68.8%, and the median movement was 15.2%. Based on the low of 360.60 in the December futures, this told him that there was a very high probability that gold would rally at least 9.4%, which is a change of $33.90 per ounce, to a price of $394.50. In addition, it told me that 50% of all moves within the last nine years rallied more than 15.2%, which for the December futures would be $54.81 per ounce to the 415.40 level.

What does all this tell you in terms of asset allocation? The extremely low technical risk/reward factor, the high historical probability of the move going to at least 394.50, and the fundamental factors all supported taking a long position on October 27. When all the factors are strongly in favor of a position like this, then it is time to become aggressive.

This means that, in the early part of the move, you should use optimum leverage. His choice was to put approximately 10% of all my managed portfolios in gold by buying calls on the gold futures, calls on some gold stocks, and some of the gold stocks themselves (the stocks for my less risk-oriented clients). Once prices broke through the 400 level, he began scale-selling at a very substantial profit, with the intention of holding a smaller, long-term position, still highly leveraged, until the market proved him wrong.

Why did he sell at all? Because after prices reached the intermediate target level, the risk/reward of holding the position increased substantially. The justification for staying involved at this point has to be a conviction that the long-term trend will keep going up. He held a smaller long position with a portion of profits, and guess what? He was wrong and lost the money. Although he was dumbfounded at the fact that gold failed to sustain its rally, his principles of money management saved me.

Let me tie this process directly to the principles of his business philosophy.

First, by using leverage and by picking a buy spot that allowed a small loss as an exit point, he did not expose capital to a high degree of risk. If by some odd circumstance, prices had failed back below the trend change confirmation point, then he could have most likely closed the position with a loss of at most 1% to 2% in his accounts. Then, if it rallied again, he could still afford to take another position. In short, he set the trade up to preserve capital.

Second, when prices reached the target level, he took enough profits to lock in a substantial gain in accordance with the goal of consistent profitability. Third, he used a portion of profits to hold a long position in the pursuit of superior returns. He was wrong in the long-term call, but he still ended up net profitable on his overall position. In my mind, that's successful speculating through smart money management. By allocating capital according to the risk of involvement and by setting preliminary exit points to lock in your profits, and by using only a portion of profits to pursue the larger gains, you'll stay at the table even when you lose some hands.

Allocating Capital

Unfortunately, there is no simple formula to plug into a computer that will tell you the best way to allocate capital in the markets. For example, I can't take my historical data and buy the stocks that make up the Dow Industrial and Transports averages according to some linear risk relationship. To do so would be to defy the nature of the markets. What you have to do is make a judgment call based on the widest context of knowledge possible, combining all aspects of your experience to form your best estimate of coming events.

Suppose we were in a strong bull market that had already exceeded its extent and duration medians. Inflation was at 2%; the world was at peace with no potential conflict in sight; corporations, in general, had little debt and high earnings; and every major country had a balanced budget, little or no debt, and operated on a free, gold based banking system. Nice thought, isn't it? In such a case, you would obviously want to be 100%o invested.

In effect, what you do is build a risk assessment scoreboard that tabulates all the driving market forces and weigh each factor separately to decide how much and in what way to put capital at risk. If you choose to invest at all, then you use the same facts as a context to choose those instruments that are most likely to achieve your goals.

What I've said so far is all very general, so let me get more specific. When you are assessing the risk of being involved in the stock market, you have to ask yourself the following questions:

1. What is the long-term trend? Is it up, is it down, is it drawing lines, or is it changing?

2. How does the current long-term trend fit within the context of history in terms of extent and duration? Is it young, old, or middle-aged?

3. What is the intermediate trend, and where does it fit within the context of history?

4. What does Dow Theory say about the current market? Are there divergences? What does the volume tell you? Is breadth moving with the trend?

5. What do the moving averages say-buy, sell, or hold?

6. Do oscillators tell you that the market is overbought, oversold, or in the middle of a move?

   What is the health of the economy?

   a. Where is inflation and what is the Fed's policy toward it? What are the levels of national, civil, corporate, and private debt? What is the rate of growth of credit availability as measured by free reserves? What is the rate of growth of the money supply? Where are interest rates? How are the markets receiving new issues of government securities?

b. How strong is the dollar relative to foreign currencies, and what is the likelihood that it could be debased? How strong are the yen and the Deutsche mark and are those governments likely to take action to protect them?

c. What is the prevailing attitude of the American consumer: produce and save, borrow and spend, or somewhere in between?

d. What economic sectors are strong? Which ones are weak'? Are any stock groups driving the market, giving it the appearance of health when in fact the tide could quickly turn at the slightest bad news?

e. What potential problems exist that could cause a sudden change of the economic climate?

7. What predominant fallacies exist that can be used to advantage, especially when the market changes?

Once you answer these questions, you then have the basis to decide when, where, and how much money to invest in the markets. And when you choose to make your move, you've got to do it in a very disciplined way. That's where rules come in, the subject of the next chapter.

Conclusion to Part I: Putting It All Together

There you have it, from the ground up. What I've presented so far is the essential knowledge that has helped make me money throughout my career. I gave you a brief history, and then showed you the knowledge I picked up along the way.

The common thread to everything I've presented so far is that it is what I consider to be basic, essential information and principles. I think if you apply these basic ideas and develop your unique style of market participation, the information will work for you, too.

If you believe in essentials and integrate your approach to trading with principles that stand the test of time, you'll be able to adapt to ever changing market conditions. As opposed to changing your hat on short-term strategies that change as the market changes, a principled approach will keep on working.

If you define your business philosophy and stick to it, you'll achieve focus in your work; you'll avoid getting off track. More specifically, if you preserve capital and shoot for consistent profits instead of the big hit, you'll avoid blowing out like so many traders do.

If you study Dow Theory, you'll gain more insight into the markets-all markets-than you will by studying any other theory of market behavior that I know of. You'll learn that market movement are largely a psychological phenomenon. Unpredictable in absolute terms, but highly predictable concerning probabilities.

If you understand trends, what they are and when they change, you'll be equipped with knowledge that will save you countless hours of study. You'll be able to avoid moving in and out of markets arbitrarily and instead trade with the trend.

If you understand technical analysis, its merits and its pitfalls, you'll be able to use it as a powerful tool to aid your market-timing decisions. If you keep your technical observations to a few essential ones, you'll keep your mind free of the extraneous clutter that paralyzes many market technicians. If you understand some simple basics of economics, including how money and credit affect the business cycle, you'll be able to predict the effects of government interference in the marketplace and make money with the knowledge.

If you learn to manage your money, limiting involvement according to the associated risk, you'll be able to stay at the table, year after year.

And if you follow the rules, you'll achieve consistency in reaching your trading goals-the hallmark of every good trader with staying power.

But as I have said before, knowledge alone is not enough. I've taught many people most of the ideas I have presented so far, yet all but five of them lost money. But it wasn't the knowledge that was at fault. It was the people, specifically their inability to put the knowledge into practice consistently. All of the people I trained were capable of making money, all of them could recognize when they violated a rule or deviated in their thinking from the principles I taught them. But they just kept on making the same mistakes over and over again.

Trading Rules and the Reasons Behind Them

Many people make the mistake of thinking that market behavior is truly predictable. Nonsense, Trading in the markets is an odds game, and the object is to always keep the odds in your favor. Like any other odds game, to win, you've got to know the rules and stick to them. Unlike other games, however, the single biggest reason that rules are necessary is to keep a check on your emotions. Assuming you have the knowledge you need to take a position with confidence, the hard part is executing the trade correctly. That's what the rules are for.

There are so many factors affecting market behavior that, with just a little mental energy, you can twist and distort them, even if only slightly, and rationalize yourself into taking unwarranted risks or closing a position too early or too late.

Just recently, on an S&P futures trade, I went short 10 minutes after the opening with a stop set 5 ticks above the day's high. In the next 30 minutes, the market went down about ten ticks from where I sold them and then looked like it might rally. I did not have a clear buy back signal on the trade at all, but, emotionally, I didn't want the small profit to turn into a loss, and I had my assistant buy them back at a 10-tick profit ($250 per contract).

Just 15 minutes later, the market broke down two full handles (a handle on the S&P futures is one full point, which is 20 ticks or $500 per contract). If I had followed the rules, I would have made five times more profit than I did. My thinking process was something like, "This market looks like it is going to rally, so I better bail out and take the profit while I have the chance." But that was just a rationalization which was shielding my fear of being wrong in the trade. The market did, in fact, rally just a little bit, but it never even approached my stop-point where the market would prove I was wrong.

The purpose of rules is to make market executions as objective and consistent as humanly possible. Without them, you'll end up imposing your wishes on your trading decisions and, nine times out of ten, your hopes will fly in the face of market action. The purpose of this chapter is to outline the major trading rules and the reasons behind them. I'll also discuss a few ways to lose money that you don't hear people talk about very much.

THE RULES DEFINED

Rule Number 1: Trade with a plan and stick to it.

Before you make any trade, it is essential that you know your objective and how you intend to reach it. This means not only identifying the risk/reward but also defining all possible courses the market might take and then defining your response. In other words, you have to know, before you ever enter the trade, all the possible outcomes. Confusion is your biggest enemy during a trade; it will cause you anguish and emotional turmoil as the trade progresses. But confusion, by definition, comes from ignorance, from not understanding what is going on or how to respond to it. The main thing you have to ask yourself in forming your plan is where, timewise, your interest is in making the trade. That is, you have to decide if you are taking the position as a day-trade (open and close the position within the day), a short term trade (held for days to weeks), a swing trade (held weeks to months), or a long-term investment (held months to years).

This decision determines which trend you focus your concentration on and therefore where you set your stops (see Rule Number 3). Once you decide, then identify all possible scenarios regarding the price movement and determine what your response to each situation will be. Specifically, determine where you will place your stops, price objectives to take profits or to increase the size of the position, and so on.

There are sometimes sources of confusion you can't control. For example, one day, while trading my personal account I was long 40 or so stocks, in lots of 2000 or more. I owned calls on the indexes. I had futures positions. I was trading very, very intensely. Then suddenly everything went black.

No, some lunatic didn't come in and knock me on the head. The power went out. We had a backup system, but it failed too.

Somehow, the phones were connected to the electrical system, so even they didn't work.

Now, I'm dealing with several exchanges, several different brokers, and I don't know what the hell is happening on the market. I ran out into the hallway and down the stairs, fumbling in my pocket, trying to find my cell phone I didn't even have the numbers to the pits I was trading in because I had direct lines to them in my office.

So there I was, out in the middle of the street on a strangers cell phone, closing my positions in a panic. Can you imagine calling directory assistance and asking for the number of the S&P futures pit in Chicago? It's funny now, but it was awful then. And, as Murphy's Law would have it, the markets had moved against me. Now that's a kind of confusion you can't control, but you may want to make sure your system has a double back-up.

Rule Number 2: Trade with the trend. "The trend is your friend!"

This is probably the most well-known rule of all. But as simple as it seems, it is easier to violate than you might think. Remember, there are three trends-the short-term, the intermediate term, and the long-term. Each trend is moving all the time and may be going in a direction opposing the other two. The short-term trend changes more rapidly and more often than the intermediate trend, and the intermediate trend changes more rapidly and more often than the long-term trend.

Know which trend you are involved in and its correlation with the other two. Identify, using the 1-2-3 change of trend criterion, the point at which the trend has reversed. If the market hits that price- get out! Also, watch for 2B patterns and other technical indicators that can give you an earlier indication of a probable trend reversal.

Rule Number 3: Use stop loss orders whenever practical.

Before opening a trade, you should know the point at which the market proves you are wrong. One of the hardest things for many traders is to close the trade when the market hits that point. One way to avoid this problem is to trade with stop loss orders. A stop order is one which converts to a market order when the price stated in the stop order is reached.

If you are trading in size, you must use mental stops. If you put huge stop orders in, then you can be sure the locals will hit them if they can.

So, once you open a position, you should place a second order to close the position at a stop. The exact way to do this depends on what trend you are involved in. As a general rule, stop orders are valid until the close on the day you place them. But you can place a stop order with the addendum "good 'til cancel," or GTC, which means that the order is good until you cancel it.

In fact, you have to watch both yourself and your broker when you place any order. My good friend, Tyler, who is a trader, tells me about people who call up and say things like, "Sell me 500 IBM at the market." So John replies, "Mmm . . . sell me, that means you're a buyer, you want me to sell to you 500 IBM?" And, of course, the customer impatiently replies, "No, no, no, I'm a seller!"

But Tyler is right. When you "buy puts," you're short. When you sell them, you're long. "Get me 10 December S&Ps at the market," doesn't mean anything. Words have a definite meaning, especially when you're placing an order in the markets, so make sure you get it right and make sure your broker understands you.

Rule Number 4: When in doubt, get out!

Another way of stating this rule is that when you are evaluating your positions, every long position you hold should be a buy today, and every short position you hold should be a sell today. It also means that you should never enter a position without confidence.

It is only natural to experience a little bit of fear or anxiety when your money is on the line, and by no means should you close a position every time you feel an inkling of doubt. But if changing conditions start to pile the odds against you and you are plagued with nagging doubt and uncertainty, then close the position.

This rule also has a second meaning. There is a fine line between fear and justifiable doubt. It may sound harsh, but if, because of fear, every position you take fills you with doubt and uncertainty, then get out of the markets! You have no business trading if you can't trade with confidence, at least most of the time. Chronic fear and doubt will take a dreadful toll on you physically, emotionally, and probably financially. It's nothing to be ashamed of; it's just a personality trait that is not conducive to being successful in the markets.

The single best way to avoid doubt during a trade is to have all the possible information you can on your side. Sometimes, though, even that is not enough.

I was told a story about a very wealthy man who dealt with a takeover analyst and usually did very well by him. The analyst had been talking about several stocks as a buy: Northwest Airlines and Cessna among them, both potential takeover stocks at the time. One day, the rich man got a call from the analyst, who said, "I just got the scoop, this thing is on. Buy the plane."

The rich man proceeded to go out and buy 400,000 shares of Northwest Airlines at $60 per share. That's $24 million worth of stock. The next day, the stock went to $59, then to $58. The rich man called the analyst.

"What's going on here, I thought the deal was on?"

The analyst was very busy, "Yep, yep, it's still a go . . . real busy. . . gotta move," and he hangs up.

Within the next two days, the stock went to $55, and the rich man called again. This time the analyst wasn't so busy.

The rich man asks, "When is this thing going to happen?" "Day after tomorrow."

"At what price?" confusion in the rich man's voice. "Above the market."

"I don't get it then," says the dumfounded rich man, "the stock's down five bucks, at $55." The analyst is surprised: "What do you mean, $55, Cessna is at $24!"

"Cessna! . . . CESSNA!"

"Yeah, Cessna! I told you to buy the plane, " says the analyst in shock. And the rich said, "But Northwest flies, too!"

The rich man blew out his position, losing 2 million dollars. All along, his doubts were justified. One more story to verify the rule, "When in doubt, get out!"

Rule Number 5: Be patient. Never overtrade.

Neel used to say that there were usually three or four excellent trading opportunities per year in any given market, including individual stocks. Neel was a speculator; he traded primarily in the intermediate term. But the essence of his point applies to every trend. You can flip a coin and say, "heads long, tails short," and trade one hundred times a day if you want to. But if you do, the only way you're going to win is through sheer luck. The way to make money is to watch the markets you are interested in and wait until as many factors as possible are in your favor before taking a position. For example, in day-trading the S&P futures, there is usually a maximum of two or three excellent trading opportunities each day. Sometimes there are none.

Each market index, each stock, and each commodity has its own unique pace, rhythm, and trading characteristics. Don't trade until you feel familiar with the price action of your market(s) and then wait for opportunities that promise large profits if you are right and small losses if you are wrong. Observe, watch patiently, and when all the factors come into play in your favor, act without hesitation.

Another aspect of this rule is that, if you are trading just in your own account, it is prudent to limit yourself to under ten stocks if you are active in the stock market, or to under five commodities if you are trading in the futures. The biggest reason for this is a simple matter of focus.

How many phone numbers do you know off the top of your head? Maybe as many as two or three. Well, if it's that hard to remember phone numbers, imagine trying to maintain the intensity required to stay on top of more than ten or so trades at once. Awareness of your positions and what they are doing is key to performing well. For most of us, thinking about five things at once is plenty of challenge.

Rule Number 6: Let your profits run; cut your losses short.

Of all the trading rules, this is the most important, most commonly stated, and the most frequently violated rule of them all.

The market is like a courtroom where you are the accused innocent until proven guilty. That is, when you initiate a trade, you have to assume that you are right until the market proves you wrong. It proves you wrong when the price hits your stop, or your mentally chosen exit point, which is as absolute as a Supreme Court ruling no appeal is possible, your freedom to act is gone, you must close out the position.

When you are right, you have to "Let freedom reign!" When you trade on a one to three risks/reward criterion, then as a general rule you should either lose one or win at least three, as I described in an earlier chapter. The exceptions are covered by Rule Number 7.

In a sense, Rule Number 6 is a restatement of all the rules covered so far. If you have a plan, then you know when to take profits, when to double up on a position, and when to close out. If you trade with the trend, then your loss limits are objectively definable by the change of trend criterion. If you trade with stops, you will automatically cut your losses short. If you trade with confidence, you are unlikely to take profits too early. If you don't overtrade, you will both minimize losses and stand a better chance of catching the winners and riding them out. If you understand "Let your profits run; cut your losses short," then you've rolled at least four rules into one-good mental economics.

Rule Number 7: Never let a profit run into a loss. (Or always take a free position if you can.)

This is a tough one because you have to define "profit" in your trading terms. To generalize the rule, consider it in terms of the 1 to 3 risks/reward context. If you are up 2 to 1, then Rule 6 says to let your profits run. But if the price trend reverses and you end up getting stopped out, then you've violated Rule 7! What are you supposed to do?

What I recommend is that any time you are up two to one on a trade, raise your stop, even if just mentally, slightly above cost and take the free position! In a sense, this gives you a zero risk/reward relationship. You have everything to gain and nothing to lose. If the trade continues going your way and reaches the 1 to 3 objective, then close out one-half or one-third of the position and raise your stop to lock in a two to one profit on the rest of the position. If the trade continues to go your way, then you can move your stop to lock in higher and higher levels of profits. And if you are playing the long term, depending on the exact nature of the market, you might even want to expand the size of your position at strategically selected points.

Rule Number 8: Buy weakness and sell strength. Be just as willing to sell as you are to buy.

This rule is primarily applicable to speculating and investing, and to a smaller degree in short-term trading. It is a corollary to Rule 2, trading with the trend. If you are speculating on the intermediate trend, the way to maximize profit potential is to sell during minor rallies and buy during minor sell-offs. If you are investing in the long-term trend, you should sell during intermediate rallies in bear markets and buy during intermediate sell-offs in bull markets.

The same reasoning holds true for adding to a profitable position in either the intermediate or long-term trend. Ideally, of course, you want to try to sell near minor rally highs and buy near minor sell-off lows when speculating in bear and bull markets, respectively; and sell near intermediate highs and buy near intermediate lows when speculating in bear markets and investing in bull markets, respectively. The 2B criterion is excellent for employing this strategy in many cases.

Many market participants are either predominantly bulls or bears and tend always to be long or always be short. In fact, most market participants avoid playing the short side like a plague. This is a big mistake that defies the nature of a market action. If "the trend is your friend," then playing both sides of the market is the best way to maintain a successful and lasting personal relationship. Any adept long-side player has, at least implicitly, the knowledge to play the short side-all he has to do is use converse reasoning. And when playing the short side, profits can accrue more quickly because downside movements occur faster than upside movements.

Rule Number 9: Be an investor in the early stages of bull markets. Be a speculator in the latter stages of bull markets and bear markets.

An investor is a person looking for a long-term return and an income flow from the placement of capital in the market. The investor's concern is primarily with earnings, dividends, and equity appreciation.

A speculator, on the other hand, is primarily concerned with price movement and how to profit from it. It looked at from a risk/reward standpoint, the best time to be an investor is at the early stages of bull markets because, from every fundamental dimension, the chances for growth are the best.

As the market ages, entering the third, fourth, and later legs, your emphasis on price levels should become more predominant, and the prudent market player will turn to speculation. The progression of a bull market induced by credit expansion is such that, at some point, value appreciation ends and price inflation begins as businesses compete with more dollars for scarce resources.

In bear markets, it is always prudent to speculate. By definition, it is impossible to be an "investor" if you are playing the short side. Long-term selling in bear markets is a means of profiting from investment liquidation; it is not investing per se. That aside, the best way to play bear markets is by moving in and out of the market, playing the short side during primary legs and the long side during secondary corrections. Bear markets are shorter than bull markets, and the primary swings in bear markets move similarly in extent, but shorter in duration than in bull markets.

If you manage your money carefully, you can make similar percentage profits in bear markets in a shorter time with no more, and perhaps even less, risk than on the upside in bull markets. By the nature of the business cycle, you'll never see a "Black Monday" on the upside, so in that sense, bear markets are safer.

Rule Number 10: Never average a loss-don't add to a losing position.

"Averaging down" is nothing more than a rationalization either to avoid admitting being wrong or to hope to recover losses against all odds. It is called "averaging down" because it is a process of adding to a losing position such that the net percentage loss on the entire position is less than it would be if the losses were calculated by the price on the opening trade. The rationalization takes the form of "This stock (bond, future, whatever) is going up (down). I'm losing money now, but if I add to the position, then I'm getting a bargain and I'll end up making lots of money!"

Rule 10 is really just a corollary of Rule 6-cut your losses short. But averaging down is such a common error that it deserves its own "don't" rule to remind you that it is an error.

There are cases. However, that may at first appear like averaging down, but aren't. For example, if you are looking for an intermediate shorting opportunity in a bear market, I've already said that the best time to go short is a minor rally. Assuming that the stock market has been down four days in a row at what looks like the beginning of a primary leg in a bear market, a good way to short is to sell the market on the first up day. If the market is up two days, then the odds of its being up the third day are relatively low so that you could increase the size of the position on the second up day. If it is up the third day, then the odds of its being up a fourth are less than 5% so that you could short again. But if the market is up four days in a row, then there is a strong possibility that the intermediate trend is, in fact, going up, and it's time to close the position.

The difference between this strategy and averaging a loss is that you have a plan and a point at which you admit that you are wrong. Part of the plan would include an evaluation of the extent of each daily move as well as the number of days. From the outset, you would consider not only the number of days, but you would also have established an exit point regarding the price level that would prove you wrong. Averaging down is without limits, and closing the position becomes a subjective, emotional decision.

Rule Number 11: Never buy just because the price is low. Never sell just because the price is high.

Unlike shopping at a grocery store for fruit, there is no such thing as a "bargain" when it comes to trading. Either a trade is good, or it isn't; the price of the instrument has almost nothing to do with it. The only time price comes into play are if you simply can't afford a position because of margin requirements, or if there are, by comparison, other trades available with greater leverage and equal or better risk/ reward ratios.

Avoid thinking in terms like, "This thing is at historical lows, it just can't go any lower!" or "This thing just can't go any higher, I've got to sell it!" The fact is, unless you see some sign of a change of trend, the chances are that the trend will continue. When a market is at historical highs or lows, but there is no sign of a change of trend, my advice is to leave it alone and wait for signs of a change of trend. Trade with the trend and be patient.

Rule Number 12: Trade only in liquid markets.

A lot of people who live in the Northeast right now might tell you that they live in a $500,000 house. But what they mean is that they either paid $500,000 for their house or had it appraised at $500,000 a couple of years ago when they got a second mortgage. In truth, right now the market is glutted with homes offered for $500,000, and there are no buyers to speak of the market is almost entirely illiquid. That $500,000 figure may work on a financial statement for the time being, but it has nothing to do with market value.

The same thing can happen to you if you trade in illiquid or "thin" markets. Prices can change very rapidly, moving right through your stops so fast that you lose perhaps twice as much as you planned on. So avoid thin, illiquid markets. Trade the front month in the commodities and currencies, and the active, high-volume stocks and options.

Rule Number 13: Never initiate a position in a fast market.

This is a rule for upstairs traders-people who rely on electronic information systems for the latest price quote. A fast market is one in which transactions are occurring so fast on the floor of the exchange that the people recording the transactions can't keep up with the pace of the price changes. It is a formal declaration made on the floor as a warning to participants who trade by watching the latest print on a screen.

In other words, in a fast market, what you see on the screen is not necessarily what you get. It can be sorely tempting to buy a breakout or sell a break into a fast market. You watch prices skyrocketing or plunging, and those dollar signs start appearing in your head.

One new trader in my office who didn't believe this rule sold the S&P futures into a fast market break. His fill was 16 ticks ($400 per contract) below where he placed his market order. Even then, according to the screen, he was up 16 ticks on the trade when he placed the buyback order. His fill was ten ticks above where he sold them-a $250 per contract loss on the trade. And if this wasn't lesson enough, he made the same mistake on the following day and got burned again. I don't think he'll ever trade a fast market again. Your trade is only as good as the information you base it on. In a fast market, the information is unreliable, so DON'T TRADE!

Rule Number 14: Don't trade on the basis of "tips." In other words, "trade with the trend, not your friend." Also, no matter how strongly you feel about a stock or other market, don't offer unsolicited tips or advice.

Just in terms of odds, when you consider the hundreds of thousands of people involved in the markets, what do you think the chances are that one of your acquaintances knows something that the rest of the world doesn't? If he or she does know something, then the chances are that it is "inside" information, and trading on inside information is illegal.

But 999 times out of 1000, the so-called "tip" is just someone else's opinion. Henry Clasing, in his book The Secrets of a Professional Futures Trader, points out that consistent winners tell virtually no one the details of their activities in the marketplace, while consistent losers "tell virtually anyone who will listen to the details of their market activities, to the point of campaigning for their point of view.'" Psychologically, people who are eager to give out tips are probably seeking recognition and admiration. For sure, they aren't doing you a favor. So, if you get a tip, my advice is to say "Thanks, but no thanks."

Just as you shouldn't listen to tips, you shouldn't offer them. It may be an admirable thing to want to help your friends out, but if you have a friend who trades, exchange ideas and discuss trading tactics in general. If you want to be a good friend, then don't make recommendations; your friend has a mind-let him or her use it. '

The main point of this rule is that there is never a good substitute for your own judgment. If you don't have enough confidence to trade based on your own judgment, then don't trade. Follow the trend, not your friend.

Rule Number 15: Always analyze your mistakes.

A losing trade isn't necessarily a mistake, and a mistake isn't necessarily a losing trade. You can make a good trade and lose money, or you can make a mistake and still make money. If you follow the rules and lose, then just let it go; you don't need to analyze it. Say to yourself, "Oh well," and move on to the next trade. But if, for example, you close out a position too early and then watch your would-be profits keep coming in, think about what you have done.

The most important reason to analyze your mistakes is that mistakes and failures are always the best teachers; they reinforce the fact that you should always follow the rules. If you can truly and honestly identify the reasons you make a mistake, then your chances of making it again are much less.

Most often, mistakes are rooted not in ignorance, but fear: fear of being wrong, fear of feeling humiliated, and so forth. To trade well, you have to conquer fear; and to conquer fear, you first have to admit having it, which means admitting your mistakes and analyzing them. I'll go into this in much more detail in the final part of the book.

Rule Number 16: Beware of "Take unders."

I got a call one day from a friend of mine who was on the board of a major company. "David," he said, "XYZ just agreed to merge with ABC. You gotta buy XYZ; it's a sure bet."

"Fred," I said, "is this legal, you telling me this?"

"Absolutely! We don't have anything to do with either company, and they've already made the announcement; it just hasn't made the wires yet."

So I looked at the price of XYZ, which was at $6 per share, and I bought a small position. Two weeks later, the companies merged . . . ABC bought out XYZ at the agreed upon price, $4.50 per share! I lost on the trade and dubbed it "a take under."

I guess this was the second time I traded on a tip, and it was the last. It was the only time I ever got a tip that came true. There was a takeover, but it was a take under. Since then, I've always shied away from alleged "takeover stocks."

Rule Number 17: Know and follow the Rules!

For every trading rule, there are probably five known ways to break it, and no doubt, traders will find a few more ways as time goes on. I've listed eighteen rules, so by that reasoning, there are at least ninety ways to break them. And, each time you break a rule, that's one more way to lose money.

THE 85% RULE

No one is 100% all the time. All kinds of things can distract you. A fight with your spouse or loved one. A call from a friend like the one I mentioned at the beginning of the chapter. There are all kinds of distractions.

For example, in 2016, I got invited to go to Chicago to make a speech. I was on the platform with some pretty heavy hitters, and a market maker named Gary Knight. As an aside, during the QA session, a member stood up and said, "I want to address the market maker. All the rules on the exchange favor the market makers who own seats."

Without hesitation, Gary said, "Yes."

"I don't think it's fair!" said the guy in the audience.

"Buy a seat," said Gary, "they're currently going for $250,000."

Remember, the rules favor the floor traders; that's how they make their living.

Anyway, there I was on the podium. I was a bear at the time, and I had hit a nice home run in January. The market had rallied and was drawing a line. I was looking for another opportunity to go short, and I had been waiting for the break for a couple of months. As luck would have it, the market broke the day I left.

The point is that, if you want to make a living in the market, you have to be as close to 100% mentally, physically, and emotionally as possible. And in my estimate, if you can average being at the 85% level, you will do well.

So when you trade, be prepared to lose money in ways you never dreamed of. At some point, when you're right on top of the market when you're poised and ready to hit that home run, you'll fight with your spouse, a family member will die, something will happen that you never expected.

Shoot for 100%, but be satisfied with 85%; that's the reality of it.

www.ingramcontent.com/pod-product-compliance
Lightning Source LLC
Chambersburg PA
CBHW050204230526
45470CB00001B/226